Junior Recitations

A Collection of Exercises,
Dialogues, and Single Pieces,
Suitable for Junior Meetings and
Public Entertainments

By Amos R. Wells

Number 1

First Fruits Press
Wilmore, Kentucky
c2015

Junior recitations : a collection of exercises, dialogues and single pieces, suitable for junior meetings and public entertainment, by Amos R. Wells.

First Fruits Press, ©2015
Previously published: Boston and Chicago: United Society of Christian Endeavor, ©1922.

ISBN: 9781621713807 (print), 9781621713814 (digital)

Digital version at http://place.asburyseminary.edu/christianendeavorbooks/15/

For all other uses, contact:

First Fruits Press
B.L. Fisher Library
Asbury Theological Seminary
204 N. Lexington Ave.
Wilmore, KY 40390
http://place.asburyseminary.edu/firstfruits

Wells, Amos R. (Amos Russel), 1862-1933.
    Junior recitations : a collection of exercises, dialogues and single pieces, suitable for junior meetings and public entertainment / by Amos R. Wells ; number 1.
    146 pages ; 21 cm.
    Wilmore, Ky. : First Fruits Press, ©2015.
    Includes index.
    Title vignette
    Reprint. Previously published: Boston : United Society of Christian Endeavor, ©1922.
    ISBN: 9781621713807 (pbk.)
    1. Recitations. I. Title.
PN4271 .W4 2015

Cover design by Jonathan Ramsay

asburyseminary.edu
800.2ASBURY
204 North Lexington Avenue
Wilmore, Kentucky 40390

First Fruits
THE ACADEMIC OPEN PRESS OF ASBURY SEMINARY

First Fruits Press

The Academic Open Press of Asbury Theological Seminary

204 N. Lexington Ave., Wilmore, KY 40390

859-858-2236

first.fruits@asburyseminary.edu

asbury.to/firstfruits

Junior Recitations

A Collection of Exercises, Dialogues,
and Single Pieces, Suitable for
Junior Meetings and Public
Entertainments

By
Amos R. Wells

Number 1

United Society of Christian Endeavor
Boston and Chicago

PREFACE.

THIS book of recitations for Junior societies is, in one point at least, different from all books of recitations with which I am acquainted. I refer to the directions for speaking prefixed to each piece. Much thought has been spent upon this unique feature, and I trust that these directions will be found to be not only workable and varied, but helpful in interpreting the spirit of the recitations to the speakers themselves, and to the children that listen.

It will be seen that the selections cover with fulness all the various holidays, anniversaries, and special occasions such as New Years, Christmas, Thanksgiving, Fourth of July, the harvest season, Children's Day, Valentine's Day, Easter, and so on, and that at the same time a large number of recitations and exercises are suitable for use at any time. The great importance of those topics has led me to pay special attention to temperance and missionary recitations and exercises.

The book contains quite a number of original exercises never published before. For permission to use the work of others I am grateful to the authors and to their publishers. I have obtained this permission whenever I could learn the address of author or publisher, and have given full credit in connection with the piece; but many of these poems were found floating about through periodical literature, and had long ago lost all trace of their parentage. In some of these I have ventured to make slight corrections, feeling sure that they were not as originally written.

Many poems are equally suitable for various occasions, and I have added at the close of the volume a full cross index, which will assist in the use of the book.

It remains to say that if this collection finds favor, it will be followed in time by others made upon the same plan.

Amos R. Wells.

Boston, Mass., July, 1899.

CONTENTS.

CONTENTS.

CONTENTS.

CONTENTS.

JUNIOR RECITATIONS.

WRITE IT.

This is best used as an exercise for five boys or girls. The key line, " Where there's drink, there's danger," should be repeated in concert by all five, throughout. The first speaker will hold up at the proper place a slate on which the sentence is boldly written; the second, a little wooden gallows bearing the same inscription; the third, a ballot similarly marked; the fourth, a toy ship with these words on its sails; the fifth holds a red paste-board heart carrying the same legend.

Write it on the workhouse gate,
Write it on the schoolboy's slate,
Write it on the copy-book,
That the young may often look : —
  " Where there's drink, there's danger."

Write it on the churchyard mound,
Where the rum-slain dead are found;
Write it on the gallows high,
Write for all the passers-by : —
  " Where there's drink, there's danger."

Write it in the nation's laws,
Blotting out the license clause;
Write it on each ballot white,
So it can be read aright : —
  " Where there's drink, there's danger."

Write it on our ships that sail,
Borne along by storm and gale ;
Write it large in letters plain,
Over every land and main : —
   " Where there 's drink, there 's danger."

Write it over every gate,
On the church and halls of state,
In the hearts of every band,
On the laws of every land : —
   " Where there 's drink, there 's danger."
  — *Frances E. Willard, who wanted every boy
and girl to commit these words to memory.*

CHEER UP.

Let a boy recite this, with the exception of the "cheer
up." For this, train a company of girls, who will sit in the
front row, and come in at the proper places with their
birdlike chorus.

A little bird sings, and he sings all day —
   " Cheer up ! Cheer up ! Cheer up ! "
No matter to him if the skies are gray —
   " Cheer up ! Cheer up ! Cheer up ! "
He flies o'er the fields of waving corn,
   And over the ripening wheat ;
He answers the lark in the early morn
   In cadences cheery and sweet ;
And only these two little words he sings —
   " Cheer up ! Cheer up ! Cheer up ! "
A message to earth which he gladly brings —
   " Cheer up ! Cheer up ! Cheer up ! "

He sings in a voice that is blithe and bold —
  "Cheer up! Cheer up! Cheer up!"
And little cares he for the storm or cold —
  "Cheer up! Cheer up! Cheer up!"
And when in the winter the snow comes
    down,
  And fields are all frosty and bare,
He flies to the heart of the busy town,
  And sings just as cheerily there.
He chirps from his perch on my window-sill —
  "Cheer up! Cheer up! Cheer up!"
This message he brings with a right good will —
  "Cheer up! Cheer up! Cheer up!"

This dear little messenger can but say
  "Cheer up! Cheer up! Cheer up!"
As over the housetops he makes his way —
  "Cheer up! Cheer up! Cheer up!"
O let us all learn from this wise little bird
  A lesson we surely should heed :
For if we all uttered but one bright word
  The world would be brighter indeed!
If only earth's children would blithely say,
  "Cheer up! Cheer up! Cheer up!"
How jolly a world would be ours to-day!
  "Cheer up! Cheer up! Cheer up!"

THE MISSIONARY SHIP.

Get together a company of children as large as you can train well. Find a toy ship fully rigged; in default of this, a large picture of a ship. The ship should be carried in clear view of the audience. The children, standing on the platform, will sing the first stanza, to the tune of "The Great Physician." They will then march from the platform to the right, singing the second stanza. When they have reached the side of the church, one of the children will recite the speech appropriate to that point of the compass, *whatever it may be.* Then they march to the next point of the compass, holding the ship aloft in the front of the procession and singing the next stanza, and so they continue until, for the fourth point of the compass, they reach the platform whence they started, and after the speech for that point of the compass sing their closing stanza.

OPENING SONG (*from the platform*).

The missionary ship is here,
   The ship of grace and glory,
The ship that travels far and near
   To bear the gospel story.

CHORUS.

Send it along, you praying band,
Send it along with gold in hand,
Send it forth to every land
   To bear the grace of Jesus.

MARCHING SONG (*to the first point of the compass*).

The missionary ship behold
   Upon its journey pressing,
Its sailors eager all, and bold
   To bring the Christian blessing.
CHORUS: Send it along, you praying band, etc.

SPEAKER (*at the north*).

The missionary ship goes north. They are waiting for it on the shores of the great Canadian forests. The Indians of Alaska are eager to receive it. It has brought untold blessings to the coasts of Greenland and Iceland. There is no country so barren or lonely that the missionary ship will not reach it, bringing warmth and cheer and joy.

MARCHING SONG (*to the next point of the compass*).

> And still the missionary ship
> Upon its course is fleeting,
> And happy songs are on the lip,
> And words of kindly greeting.

CHORUS: Send it along, you praying band, etc.

SPEAKER (*at the west*).

The missionary ship goes west. It finds there the wonderful Sunrise Empire of Japan, all ready and eager for what it brings. It finds the vast land of China, just waking up from its sleep of ages, and reaching out blindly for the light. It finds the millions of India, half starved for the bread of this world, and almost wholly starved for the Bread of Life. And everywhere among the uncounted multitudes of Asia the missionary ship scatters a peace and a joy they have never before imagined.

MARCHING SONG (*to the next point of the compass*).

> Still on and on the vessel goes
> To every eager nation,
> With light for darkness, balm for woes,
> And with the great Salvation.

CHORUS: Send it along, you praying band, etc.

SPEAKER (*at the south*).

The missionary ship goes south.   The Neglected Continent is here, South America, whose shores the noble vessel has so seldom touched.   Here are the islands of the sea, whose cannibals are fast becoming Christian saints.   Here is the Dark Continent, still groaning under the curse of slavery, and with its only hope borne on the missionary ship.

MARCHING SONG (*to the next point of the compass*).
> The sinning, suff'ring world around
> Our blessed ship is sailing,
> And where it goes, — O hear the sound ! —
> Are songs in place of wailing.

CHORUS : Send it along, you praying band, etc.

SPEAKER (*at the east*).

The missionary ship goes east.   It sails to Spain and France and Italy, and finds them bound down under heavy burdens of superstition.   It enters the lovely harbor of Constantinople, whose waters may still at any day run red with the blood of Christians murdered by the Turk.   It goes on to the Holy Land itself, and finds a false and degrading religion in possession of Bethlehem and Jerusalem.   And everywhere, even there, the missionary ship wins victories, and sets up the banner of Christ.

CLOSING SONG (*from the platform*).
> And now may God who rules the sea
> Speed onward this salvation,
> Till all to Christ have bent the knee
> In every tribe and nation.

CHORUS.

Send it along, you praying band,
Send it along with gold in hand,
Send it forth till every land
    Has learned the name of Jesus.
              — *Amos R. Wells.*

MY KINGDOM.

A pretty and appropriate accompaniment to this beautiful poem of Miss Alcott's would be a crown and a sceptre worn and carried by the little child who speaks the piece.

A little kingdom I possess,
    Where thoughts and feelings dwell,
And very hard the task I find
    Of governing it well;
For passion tempts and troubles me,
    A wayward will misleads,
And selfishness its shadow casts
    On all my words and deeds.

How can I learn to rule myself,
    To be the child I should,
Honest and brave, and never tire
    Of trying to be good?
How can I keep a sunny soul,
    To shine along life's way?
How can I tune my little heart
    To sweetly sing all day?

Dear Father, help me with the love
  That casteth out my fear;
Teach me to lean on thee, and feel
  That thou art very near;
That no temptation is unseen,
  No childish grief too small,
Since thou, with patience infinite,
  Dost soothe and comfort all.

I do not ask for any crown
  But that which all may win;
Nor try to conquer any world,
  Except the one within.
Be thou my Guide until I find,
  Led by a tender hand,
Thy happy kingdom in myself,
  And dare to take command.

—Louisa M. Alcott.

OUR NATIONAL BANNER.

This would be a very attractive recitation if spoken in
concert by several children, who carry flags and wave them
as they speak. For each stanza let the flags be used differ-
ently, *e. g.*, quietly swung to and fro in the first stanza,
waved brightly in the second, and held high in the air over
their heads with the third stanza.

O'er the high and o'er the lowly,
Floats that banner bright and holy,
  In the rays of Freedom's sun,
In the nation's heart embedded,
O'er our Union truly wedded,
  One in all, and all in one.

Let that banner wave forever,
May its lustrous stars fade never,
  Till the stars shall pale on high;
While there 's right the wrong defeating,
While there 's hope in true hearts beating,
  Truth and Freedom shall not die.

As it floated long before us,
Be it ever floating o'er us,
  O'er our land from shore to shore:
There are freemen yet to wave it,
Millions who would die to save it —
  Wave it, save it, evermore.

— Dexter Smith.

TWO TO MAKE A QUARREL.

The child who speaks this will hold up both forefingers, with the words, " Two it takes to make a quarrel," and only one forefinger with the words, " One can always end it."

There 's a knowing little proverb
  From the sunny land of Spain,
But in Northland, as in Southland,
  Is its meaning clear and plain.
Lock it up within your heart,
  Neither lose nor lend it, —
Two it takes to make a quarrel,
  One can always end it.

Try it well in every way,
  Still you 'll find it true.

In a fight without a foe
  Pray what could you do?
If the wrath is yours alone,
  Soon you will expend it;
Two it takes to make a quarrel,
  One can always end it.

THE BARGAIN.

One of the older boys represents the uncle, and two
little girls are talking with him.

UNCLE.

Bessie, Josie, seems to me
Two small girls I chanced to see
Nid-nid-nodding in their pew.
O, I *hope* it was n't you!

BESSIE.

Well, but, uncle, don't you know,
Saturday we had to go
On that picnic?   Had to play,
O, so hard! the livelong day.

UNCLE.

I 'll forgive you, Jo and Bess,
For I really must confess —
Keep it secret, children, do! —
I was rather sleepy, too!

JOSIE.

Uncle, did *you* have to play,
O, so hard! all Saturday?

UNCLE.

No, alas! my play I shirked.
I just worked, and worked, and
    worked.
Late last night I went to bed,
And got up — a sleepy head!

BOTH GIRLS.

Well, then, uncle, I don't see
But you 're just as bad as we!

UNCLE.

Just as wicked, I 'll admit.
Are n't we all ashamed of it?
Drowsy head and sleepy face
There in Christ's own dwelling-
    place!
Come, my lassies, what d' ye say?
Let 's reform next Saturday!
You to do a little less
Of your playing, Jo and Bess;
I to wheedle from the store
Time to play a little more:
Then I 'm sure that we 'll succeed
And keep awake.

BOTH GIRLS.

Well, *we* 're agreed!
                    — *Amos R. Wells.*

ONE LETTER THROUGH THE BIBLE.

For this exercise make two J's out of pasteboard. They should be about three feet high. Back them up with wood and give each a support, so that they can stand straight on a table in front of the audience. Paint one black, and gild the other. Next make from pasteboard 25 small J's, each four inches long; or longer, if your room is large. Paint three of these black, and gild the rest. The exercise can use as many as 26 children, but you may use fewer by omitting some of the less important letters, or by giving each child two or more letters. The latter plan is to be preferred, as much of the force of the exercise lies in the number of names brought out. Hooks upon the tops of the small J's should answer to eyes projecting from the large ones, so that each child may hang his letter upon the large one as he speaks, or better, hand it to the leader who will hang it up for him.

Leader (to the audience). — It will be interesting to trace through the Bible a single letter — the letter J. (*Turning to the children.*) What is the greatest Bible name that begins with J?

First Child. — Jesus.

Second Child. — Jehovah.

Leader. — Yes, both are right, for Jesus and Jehovah are one. This great golden letter will stand for Jesus and for Jehovah. But there are many noble men and women of the Bible whose names begin with J. Can you tell us what they are?

First Child. — The first is Job, whom Jehovah tested with terrible afflictions, but who cried in the midst of them all, " I know that my Redeemer liveth."

Leader (as she puts the letter in place). — One of the earliest prophets of Jesus. Surely his letter deserves a place on this great one. And who came next?

Second Child. — Jacob, the father of the Israelites, who saw God face to face.

Leader. — Yes, and who, when he was dying, said that the sceptre should not depart from Judah "until Shiloh come." He also deserves a place. And who is third?

Third Child. — Joseph, who conducted himself so wisely in Egypt that God's children were saved from the famine.

Leader. — Yes, Joseph was one of the wisest and greatest men that have ever lived. And who stands fourth?

Fourth Child. — Jochebed, the mother of Moses, Aaron, and Miriam.

Leader. — She must have been a good mother to have such good children. Let us place her here for her own sake, and also in honor of Moses, the greatest man that ever lived, the man that wrote of Jesus, as Jesus himself said. And who came after Moses?

Fifth Child. — Joshua, the valiant soldier who conquered Canaan for the Hebrews.

Leader. — Yes, and it is especially fitting to place him here because "Joshua" is only another form of the name "Jesus." And who led Israel after Joshua?

Sixth Child. — The Judges. My letter stands for them, and also for one of the most remarkable of them, for Jephthah, who dedicated his daughter to the Lord.

Leader. — And so we place your letter upon this which stands for Jesus, the well beloved son whom

God dedicated to the good of this world. And who comes next on our list?

Seventh Child. — Jesse, the father of David, the great king of Israel.

Leader. — It is right to place his letter upon that of "great David's greater Son." And who next?

Eighth Child. — Joab, David's mighty captain.

Leader. — We place his letter upon that of the great Captain of our salvation.

Ninth Child. — And Jonathan, David's noble friend.

Leader. — As we add his letter, let us remember the Bible saying, " There is a Friend that sticketh closer than a brother." That friend is Jesus. But soon came sad division of the kingdom into Judah and Israel. There were some great kings of Judah whose names began with J.

Tenth Child. — First there is Jehoshaphat, the good king who put down idolatry and sent Bible teachers all over his kingdom.

Eleventh Child. — Then there is Joash, the young king who repaired the temple.

Tenth Child. — I think that letter should stand, also, for the kind aunt of Joash, Jehosheba, who saved him from the massacre.

Ninth Child. — And I think it should stand, too, for Jehosheba's husband, the high priest, Jehoiada, who helped the young king to rule wisely.

Leader. — It shall stand for all three.

Twelfth Child. — The last of these good kings was Josiah, who honored the Bible when it was discovered hidden in the temple.

Leader. — So it is right to place all these letters upon our letter which stands for Jesus, since they all helped to keep the Messiah's people true to the one God. During the times of these last kings there were some prophets whose names began with J.

Thirteenth Child. — There is Joel, who recorded God's promise: " I shall bring again the captivity of Judah."

Fourteenth Child. — There is Jonah, whose experience was a foreshadowing of Jesus' resurrection.

Fifteenth Child. — And there was Jeremiah, who prophesied of the Branch, of Jesus' birth, and of the massacre of the children in Bethlehem.

Leader. — That brings us to the New Testament itself. Whose letter comes first in the New Testament?

Sixteenth Child. — That of John the Baptist, who prepared the way of the Lord.

Leader. — And three of Jesus' own true disciples were joined to him by this letter, besides one false one. Who were the three?

Seventeenth Child. — There was Jude, who wrote one of the books of the New Testament, and who may have been one of our Lord's brothers.

Eighteenth Child. — There was James, the son of Zebedee, the first of the apostles to be killed, and also that James who was the head of the Church and who wrote the book of the New Testament.

Nineteenth Child. — And best of all there was John, the disciple whom Jesus loved.

Leader. — It is well to end our list of men with

this honored name. But we have room here for four more letters. There are four names of places most closely connected with Jesus, and they also begin with J.

Twentieth Child. — Judea, the province where he was born.

Twenty-first Child. — The Jordan, where he was baptized.

Twenty-second Child. — Jericho, connected with his ministry.

Twenty-third Child. — The Holy City, Jerusalem, where he died and rose from the dead.

Leader. — Here stands a black letter, which we are not willing to approach after all the glory and the beauty of the golden letter we have been studying; but this black letter, too, is in the Bible. It stands for the worst man that ever lived. Who was he?

First Child. — Judas, who betrayed Jesus.

Leader. — The letter is black enough now, but once it was golden like the others. Sin drove all the sunshine and the beauty out of his life. Now let us hang upon this black letter two others that will represent all the evil in the Old Testament, as it represents all the evil in the New. Who was the most wicked woman in the Old Testament?

Twenty-fourth Child. — Jezebel, the cruel and idolatrous queen.

Leader. — And who was the most wicked man of the Old Testament?

Twenty-fifth Child. — Jeroboam, who divided the

kingdom, introduced idolatry among the Hebrews, and set an example for all the evil kings that followed him.

Leader. — Yes, and those will be enough, for the Bible has far more to say about good people than bad ones. And now in closing let us turn again to our golden letter, and let us repeat together a great verse that gives the secret of this letter J which we have been studying.

All together. — That he may be Just, and the Justifier of him which believeth in Jesus.

— Amos R. Wells.

CHRISTMAS HAS COME AGAIN.

Let one child speak this. Back of her on the platform may stand a number of smaller children. When she comes to the words, " Christmas has come again," she stops and the smaller children take up the refrain, and so for each of the nine times the sentence occurs. Of course this "chorus" must come in with absolute promptness.

The bells in the steeples ring out the glad sound,
 Christmas has come again.
From hilltop and valley the echoes resound,
 Christmas has come again.
Day bright and happy, the sweetest of earth,
Season of charity, gladness, and mirth,
Blest festal morn of our dear Saviour's birth.
 Christmas has come again.

Unite, happy voices, in jubilant song,
 Christmas has come again.

Come, shout, little children, a glad, merry throng,
  Christmas has come again.
Let love rule all hearts on this glorious day,
And strife and resentment be banished away,
While the peace of our Saviour on earth shall
   hold sway.
  Christmas has come again.

O blest angel choir from the heavenly blue,
  Christmas has come again.
Bring to our hearts the sweet story anew,
  Christmas has come again.
Sing the sweet carol of Bethlehem's hill,
Dispelling the shadows of sorrow and ill
With glad welcome sunshine of peace and good
   will:
  Christmas has come again.
     — *Ada Simpson Sherwood.*

NO.

Get the speaker to throw all possible force into these
No's. Make them explosive. Let him fairly shout them.
The effect of the piece depends upon their vigor. Before
each "No," have him make a short pause.

  Somebody asked me to take a drink.
  What did I tell him ? What do you think ?
   I told him — *No !*

  Somebody asked me one day to play
  A game of cards ; and what did I say ?
   I told him — *No !*

Somebody laughed when I would not swear
Nor lie nor steal; but I did not care.
    I told him — *No !*

Somebody asked me to take a sail
On the Sabbath day; 't was of no avail.
    I told him — *No !*

" If sinners entice thee, consent thou not,"
My Bible said, and so on the spot
    I told him — *No !*

THREE P'S.

This is to be spoken by three boys, each of whom
carries in his hand a large letter P. The third boy carries
also a flag.

ALL THREE TOGETHER.

Ho, boys ! I'd like to say to you,
    As if I were your father,
With earnest mind and good intent,
    A word — or three words, rather.

Pluck, Purpose, Perseverance, they;
    I call them simply glorious,
For they who have and use them well
    Shall surely be victorious.

FIRST BOY.

Purpose sees something to be done
    For our own good or neighbor's.

SECOND BOY.

Pluck dares to do it, and in faith
    For the great object labors.

THIRD BOY.

(*Waving his flag at the end, and leading the boys as
they march off the platform.*)

But Pluck and Purpose both are vain,
    We learn from many a story;
'T is Perseverance wins the day,
    And leads the boys to glory.

HOW TO DO IT.

Four children — two boys and two girls, possibly — may
recite this poem, each taking a stanza in turn. They
should all bear sickles.

The fields are all white
    And the reapers are few;
We children are willing,
    But what can we do
To work for our Lord in his harvest?

Our hands are so small,
    And our words are so weak,
We cannot teach others;
    How, then, shall we seek
To work for our Lord in the harvest?

We 'll work by our prayers,
    By the pennies we bring,
By small self-denials —
    The least little thing
May work for our Lord in his harvest,

Until by and by
  As the years pass at length,
We, too, may be reapers,
  And go forth in strength
To work for our Lord in his harvest.

BEAUTIFUL WORDS.

Four girls should come forward, each with a basket on
her arm. They take turns speaking the four stanzas, but
all repeat in concert the last two lines of each stanza, at
the same time putting their hands in their baskets and
going through the motion of taking something out and
scattering it. If this is done in strict time and harmony,
it will be very effective.

'Mid the losses and the gains,
'Mid the pleasures and the pains,
'Mid the hoping and the fears,
And the restlessness of years,
We repeat this passage o'er —
We believe it more and more —
  Bread upon the waters cast
  Shall be gathered at the last.

Gold and silver, like the sands,
Will keep slipping through our hands;
Jewels, gleaming like a spark,
Will be hidden in the dark;
Sun and moon and stars will pale,
But these words will never fail:
  Bread upon the waters cast
  Shall be gathered at the last.

Soon like dust, to you and me,
Will our earthly treasures be;
But the loving word and deed
To a soul in bitterest need, —
They will not forgotten be,
They will live eternally.
    Bread upon the waters cast
    Will be gathered at the last.

Fast the moments slip away,
Soon our mortal powers decay,
Low and lower sinks the sun,
What we do must soon be done;
Then what rapture, if we hear
Thousand voices ringing clear:
    Bread upon the waters cast
    Will be gathered at the last.

WHISTLE! DON'T WHINE!

A girl should recite this, and while she is speaking let some boys, hidden behind a screen or in another room, whistle softly some merry tune. Of course it is needless to say that this suggestion is intended only for entertainments not held in any sacred place.

It is better to whistle than whine,
    It is better to laugh than to cry,
For though it be cloudy, the sun will soon shine
Across the blue, beautiful sky.

It is better to whistle than whine,
    O man with the sorrowful brow,

Let the words of the child scatter murmurs
    of thine,
  And gather its cheerfulness now.

It is better to whistle than whine,
  Poor mother, so weary with care,
Thank God for the love and the peace that
    are thine
  And the joy of thy little ones share.

It is better to whistle than whine,
  Though troubles you find in your way;
Remember that wise little fellow of mine,
  And whistle your whining away.

God bless that brave boy for the cheer
  He brought to this sad heart of mine;
When tempted to murmur, that young voice
    I hear;
  It is better to whistle than whine!

JUST FOR TO-DAY.

Four children repeat this softly, each taking a stanza in turn, and all uniting to repeat the last stanza, which sums it all up.

    Lord, for to-morrow and its needs
        I do not pray;
    Keep me, my God, from stain of sin
        Just for to-day.

    Let me both diligently work
        And duly pray;
    Let me be kind in word and deed
        Just for to-day.

Let me be slow to do my will —
    Prompt to obey;
Help me to sacrifice myself
    Just for to-day.

Let me no wrong or idle word
    Unthinking say —
Set thou a seal upon my lips
    Through all to-day.

So for to-morrow and its needs
    I do not pray,
Still **keep** me, guide me, love me, **Lord,**
    Through each to-day.
                    — *E. R. Wilberforce.*

EASTER CAROL.

A girl dressed in white, bearing in her hand an Easter lily, may speak this poem. Immediately at its close, without further announcement, the rest of the children may sing an Easter hymn. Perhaps a better way to do it would be for the speaker to recite only one stanza, then the children sing one stanza of their hymn; then the speaker repeats another stanza, followed by the second stanza of the hymn, and so on.

Sing, children, sing!
Christ has risen from the tomb!
He has glorified its gloom!
Henceforth death shall ever be
Swallowed up in victory.
    Sing, children, sing!

Sing, children, sing!
Let the strain rise loud and clear,
Send the tidings far and near!
Christ has conquered every foe!
Man's last enemy lies low!
    Sing, children, sing!

Sing, children, sing!
Jesus lives for evermore!
Shout the glad news o'er and o'er!
Tell the world, this Easter day,
Jesus lives to reign for aye!
    Sing, children, sing!
           — Emma C. Dowd.

THY NEIGHBOR.

Four children come forward, bearing a long strip of paper. They unroll it, and hold it stretched out before them as they stand in a row. On it is printed very plainly the question, "Who is my neighbor?" This question the children answer by repeating the poem, verse about, uniting on the last stanza.

Thy neighbor? It is he whom thou
    Hast power to aid and bless,
Whose aching heart and burning brow
    Thy soothing hand may press.

Thy neighbor? 'T is the fainting poor
    Whose eye with want is dim,
Whom hunger sends from door to door —
    Go thou and succor him.

Thy neighbor? 'T is that weary man,
  Whose years are at their brim,
Bent low with sickness, cares, and pain —
  Go thou and comfort him.

Thy neighbor? 'T is the heart bereft
  Of every earthly gem ;
Widow and orphan, helpless left —
  Go thou and shelter them.

Whene'er thou meet'st a human form
  Less favored than thine own,
Remember 't is thy neighbor worm,
  Thy brother or thy son.

SELF-DENIAL WEEK.

This poem is appropriate to any missionary meeting, but especially suitable when money that has been raised is to be reported. The speaker may hold a mite-box in her hand.

Self-Denial Week in the Mission Band,
As of course you readily understand,
Was planned for the purpose of giving a lift
To the mission cause by an extra gift.

" O, dear," cried Bessie, " O my ! O my !
I do n't see how *I* can self-deny.
I 've nothing to do it with at all ;
I 've scarcely a penny my own to call !
Whatever I save must be very small."

" I wonder, I wonder," cried Tom and Lou,
" What in the world *we* can ever do.
Not a cent is ours, to spend or give;
'T is as much as we all can do to live.
If we earned a little, 't would be so small
It would n't be worth our giving at all."

So the children talked; but they talked in vain,
For the leader hastened to make it plain
That the " doing without " for the Saviour's sake,
And the little sacrifice each could make,
Were the very things that they all should seek,
Just a day at a time, self-denial week.

You might never guess how it came about,
But each one found something to do without,
For their hearts in earnest they really gave,
And their best endeavors to earn and save.

Not a single member of that bright band
Had a chance to do something great and grand,
But the little things by the many wrought
Exceeded all they had hoped or thought;
And the gifts of their hands went far and wide,
That the bread of light might not be denied,
But the hungry souls might be satisfied.
If you add the littles and multiply,
You will find that they count up, by and by.
It is *keeping on*, after all, that counts,
And that brings to the treasury large amounts.

THE UNFAILING CRUSE.

Four children may recite this poem, each repeating a
stanza.   Stretch a line at the back of the platform, and
upon it, as he finishes his stanza, let each speaker hang a
card, immediately taking his seat.   Each card will sum up
the stanza he has repeated, and the four will be, in order:
" Give "; " Help "; " Heal "; " Love."

Is thy cruse of comfort failing?
  Rise and share it with another.
And through all the years of famine
  It shall serve thee and thy brother.
Love divine shall fill thy storehouse,
  Or thy handful still renew ;
Scanty fare for one will often
  Make a royal meal for two.

For the heart grows rich in giving ;
  All its wealth is living gain ;
Seeds which mildew in the garner.
  Scattered, fill with gold the plain.
Is thy burden hard and heavy?
  Do thy steps drag wearily?
Help to bear thy brother's burden ;
  God will bear both it and thee.

Numb and weary on the mountain,
  Wouldst thou sleep amidst the snow?
Chafe that frozen form beside thee
  And together both shall glow.
Art thou stricken in life's battle?
  Many wounded round thee moan ;
Lavish on their wounds thy balsam,
  And that balm shall heal thine own.

Is thy heart a well left empty?
  None but God its void can fill;
Nothing but a ceaseless fountain
  Can its ceaseless longing still.
Is the heart a living power?
  Self-entwined, its strength sinks low;
It can only live in loving,
  And by serving, love will grow.
                              — *Mrs. Charles.*

WHAT HE COULD NOT SAY.

Print the words, "Thank you," in large letters on a
sheet of pasteboard.   The speaker (boy or girl) will hold
this placard turned away from the audience until the last
line of each stanza, and then, instead of speaking the
words, will shut his or her mouth tight, turn the placard
around, and simply point to the words thereon.

I knew a boy with a busy tongue
As ever inside a bell was swung.
He had a voice to read and declaim;
But these were words that he could not frame —

| Thank you. |

Other boys, made of different stuff,
Offered a "thank you" brightly enough;
But all the time that this boy was young,
The sentence stuck like wax to his tongue —

| Thank you. |

He grew like others, far as we knew,
Yet never he in the least outgrew
The luckless habit of being dumb
When the civility ought to come —

> Thank you.

NO TIME TO PRAY.

This may be used as a recitation for one child, or, if
desired, as a recitation for six children, each repeating
a stanza in turn, and all uniting in the last stanza.

No time to pray !
O who so fraught with earthly care
As not to give to humble prayer
    Some part of day ?

No time to pray !
What heart so clean, so pure within,
That needeth not some check from sin,
    Needs not to pray ?

No time to pray !
'Mid each day's danger, what retreat
More needful than the mercy-seat ?
    Who need not pray ?

No time to pray !
Must care or business' urgent call
So press us as to take it all,
    Each passing day ?

No time to pray!
Then sure your record falleth short;
Excuse will fail you as resort
    On that last day.

What thought more drear
Than that our God his face should hide,
And say, through all life's swelling tide,
    No time to hear!

Cease not to pray;
On Jesus as your all rely.
Would you live happy, happy die?
    Take time to pray.

DO A KINDNESS.

Nine children may recite this, each of the nine taking
a couplet, and all joining in the last stanza.   If you wish,
you may give each child a letter of the words, "*A kindness*," to show in the proper order.

Do a kindness, do it well;
Angels will the story tell.

Do a kindness, tell it not;
Angel hands will mark the spot.

Do a kindness; though no story
It may grace, 't will ring in glory.

Do a kindness; though 't is small,
Angel voices sing it all.

Do a kindness; never mind!
What you lose, the angels find.

Do a kindness, small or great;
'T will come back in double weight.

Do a kindness, never fret;
No good deed has been lost yet.

Do a kindness, do it now;
Angels know it all somehow.

Do a kindness any time ;
Angels weave it into rhyme.

Kindly deeds and thoughts and words
Bless the world like songs of birds.
— *Helen Chace.*

THE COLLECTION.

Six children, five boys and one girl, sit on the platform.
One holds a singing-book in front of his face ; one pretends
to be fast asleep; one carries a big purse stuffed full; one
has a purse with a great hole in it ; one carries a large
bill-book ; the last, the girl, has in her hand a poor little
purse.   To these comes the first speaker, a girl, with a
contribution-box in her hand.   She places the box before
each of the six, speaking as she does so :

Once upon a time God sent his angel to church to
take up a collection.   No one knew that it was his
angel.   Every one thought it was only dear old
Deacon Brown.   But really it was God's angel that
passed around the box.   The angel came to Mr.
Hypocrite and said, holding the box before him :
"The Lord needs some of your money to do his
work."   But the squire was singing so hard that he

did not, or would not, see the contribution-box. He was singing " Speed away."

Then the angel passed on to the seat where sat Mr. Stupid, and found him fast asleep. " Wake up!" cried the angel. " Here is God's great work to be done, and a chance for you to have some part in it. Wake up!" But Mr. Stupid slept calmly on.

The angel passed next to the pew of Mr. Money-bags. He had a great purse stuffed full of bills, and the angel said, " God has trusted you with much wealth ; now what will you render unto the Lord for all his benefits to you? " Mr. Moneybags fumbled at his purse. It was crammed so full that he could hardly open it, and it took him a long time, but the angel was very patient, expecting a large gift. At last Mr. Moneybags got into his purse, hunted around anxiously, and brought out — a five-cent piece, which he placed in the contribution-box as if it were a fortune.

With a sigh the angel went on to the pew of Mr. Careless. " The Lord is in need, in terrible need," the heavenly messenger pleaded. " What will you do to help God's needy ones? " Mr. Careless showed the angel a great hole in his purse and shook his head. His money had slipped out, he did not know how, and he had none to give.

Next in order came the pew of Mr. Schemer, and again the angel made the plea : " For the love of Christ who died for you, have you nothing to give to Christ's work in the world? " At this Mr. Schemer looked in his big bill-book, but found nothing there except large bank-notes — no small change. **So he shook** his head, and the angel passed on.

Last of all, the angel came to a certain poor woman with a lean purse. The purse was almost empty, but it contained all the poor woman had. The angel was on the point of passing by, thinking it a pity to ask anything from one so poor, but the woman had heard what had been said to the others, and she eagerly reached forward and threw her purse into the contribution-box ; and her face looked as happy as heaven.

The second speaker comes forward bearing another contribution-box.   This speaker is a boy.   He says : —

And it happened soon that Satan came to this same set of people, and he also took up a collection.   He came to Mr. Hypocrite and stuck his contribution-box under his nose.   " What will you give to tickle your palate ? " he asked : " to pamper your appetite, to dull your brain ? "   And at once Mr. Hypocrite took down his singing-book and threw into the box his purse with all it contained.

Then Satan passed to Mr. Stupid and asked, " What will you give to be amused, to witness vile plays, to hear indecent songs ? "   And Mr. Stupid at once woke up and threw into the box his purse, with all the ready money he had.

Mr. Moneybags came next.   " What will you give," said Satan, " to make men envious, to set up a fine house, an expensive carriage, many servants, costly furniture, the most luxurious living?   What ? "   And straightway the big, fat purse went in.

Mr. Careless was next in order. "What!" exclaimed Satan, "you have let a hole come in your purse and all your money slip away! What have you now to give for the pleasures of the world?" At this Mr. Careless pulled from his pocket a promissory note, made out for a large sum and duly signed and endorsed, which he placed in the contribution-box.

With a smile of satisfaction Satan passed on to Mr. Schemer. "I saw your little device regarding small change," chuckled Satan; "but you will not play that game on me, I know. How many ten-dollar bills, how many twenty-dollar bills will you give for a good time, for fine clothes, for unnecessary things, for extravagances?" And without looking to see what was in it, Mr. Schemer threw into the box his great bill-book.

Then Satan came to the poor woman, and with one glance at her happy face he hurried by, almost dropping his box, for he saw shining upon her face something that Satan fears and hates — the love of God.

Both speakers together (holding out their boxes — the one heaped full and the other nearly empty) : —

> And so when heavenly angels plead
> For human anguish, human need,
> When He who freely gave us all
> Repeats his loving, earnest call,
> How hard our hearts, our hands how cold,
> How pitiful the gift of gold!
> And then when Satan makes demand

For time and thought, for gold and land,
At his behest who never gave
A single blessing to his slave
How glad are we to give and spend
As if the devil were our friend !
Behold these boxes !　Answer true :
Which box receives the most from you ?
　　　　　　　　— *Amos R. Wells.*

ONLY A PENNY.

Four children may speak this, each with a penny in hand, which they hold out at the close of each stanza. They may take turns repeating a verse, and all may unite on the last two lines of each stanza.　If preferred, the entire poem may be recited by one child.

" Only a penny," I heard them say.
" A penny for Jesus if given each day
Would send the gospel to every soul
Now sitting in darkness, from pole to pole.
Only a penny from every one
Who bears the name of God's own Son."

Only a penny !　How small a sum,
By the side of millions that go for rum
To ruin the bodies and souls of men,
Or the millions that end in smoke — and then,
A penny apiece from every one
Who is saved by the death of God's own Son !

Only a penny from young and old,
From the little lambs within the fold ;

From the orphaned and widowed ones who share,
With all God's poor, in the Shepherd's care.
Only a penny from every one
Who prays in the name of God's own Son.

Only a penny to show our love
To Him who left his home above
For this very work; and whose last command
Left this mission to Christians in every land.
Only a penny from every one
To send the gospel of God's own Son.

A MISSIONARY HYMN.

Four children may repeat this piece, each taking a
stanza, and all joining in the last stanza. The last four
lines should be spoken as a prayer, the children all kneel-
ing, or else raising their hands to heaven. The first child
should place hand on heart during the first four lines, and
stretch it out eagerly during the second four lines. The
second child carries a banner; the third, some seed in a
basket; the fourth, a sickle.

We bring our hearts to Jesus
　To have them freed from sin;
His precious blood will cleanse them,
　His Spirit dwell within;
Then ready for his service
　We can go forth with prayer,
To do the work he gives us
　And serve him anywhere.

We bring our hands to Jesus,
　That he may make them strong,

To fight the daily battle
  With sin and every wrong;
We 're soldiers in his army
  And pledged to serve our King.
Then let us lift his banner
  With faith unwavering.

We bring our seed to Jesus,
  The seed we want to sow,
That he may give his blessing,
  And cause each grain to grow;
We 're sowing for the harvest,
  And pray for precious corn,
To fill the Master's garner,
  Upon the happy morn.

We want to glean for Jesus,
  In fields both far and near,
To gather in the lost ones,
  The gospel news to hear;
Although he may not send us
  To work in distant lands,
We know he also serveth
  Who by his Master stands.

But if the voice of Jesus
  Should say, " Go, work to-day,"
We want to follow gladly
  To dark lands far away.
O Saviour, take us, use us,
  And make us all thine own,
Thy weak and faltering children,
  But thine, Lord — thine alone !

THE OLD WOMAN'S MONEY.

An old woman's shawl may be thrown over the shoulders
of the girl that speaks this, and she may carry in her hand
a bank-book, which she will show at the proper place.

In the top of a tenement house
   Lived a little old woman alone.
Her curtains were white as the snow,
   And her windows and looking-glass shone.
Though her back it was bent like a bow,
   Yet her mind was as keen as a briar;
And she said, " I am eighty years old,
   And my life 's going out like a fire;
It is time that my will should be made,
   For (my hard-working hands I may thank!)
I have six hundred dollars laid by,
   Safe and sound, in the Beverly Bank.
And to whom shall that money be left?
   For I never can sit down content,
If I think what so hardly was earned
   In the end will in folly be spent.
But whom that I really can trust
   And will try to do right do I know?

" There is one; 't is the red-headed boy
   Who lives down in the basement below.
He has always been kind to my cat
   When the creature of dogs was afraid;
And has driven the children away
   When with Tabby too roughly they played.

And there 's one little girl in the ' L,'
  Who, whenever we happen to meet,
With a bow, says, ' Good-day to you, ma'am,'
  So respectful and gentle and sweet.
Now a boy who is kind to a cat
  Will be kind, when he 's grown, **to his wife**;
And a girl to old women polite
  Will be lovely through all of her life.
And to-morrow my will shall be made,
  For my money 't is safe to bestow
On that nice little girl in the ' L,'
  And the boy in **the basement below."**

THE SUPERCILIOUS SEED.

The speaker should carry to the platform a large weed
held carefully behind him out of sight of the audience.
With the very last line the weed should be brought forward and shown.

A little seed lay in the ground,
  And soon began to sprout;
" Now, which of all the flowers around,"
  It mused, " shall I come out?

" The lily's face is fair and proud,
  But just a trifle cold;
The rose, I think, is rather loud,
  And then, its fashion 's old.

" The violet is very well,
  But not a flower I 'd choose;

Nor yet the Canterbury-bell —
    I never cared for blues.

" Petunias are by far too bright,
    And vulgar flowers, beside;
The primrose only blooms at night,
    And peonies spread too wide."

And so it criticized each flower,
    This supercilious seed;
Until it woke one summer hour
    And found itself — a weed.

NEW RECRUITS.

    This, of course, needs one of the older boys to recite it. If the speaker holds in his hand a whiskey bottle (empty, although it should not appear so) he may use it in effective gestures of invitation. At the close, when he changes his tone at " Stand back, ye tempters!" etc., he should dash the bottle to the floor, breaking it to pieces.

Stand back, young men!
                   Here comes a lad!
Hello, my boy! Come in; you 're welcome here!
And so you thought you 'd come and see the fun;
That 's right! boys cannot always stay in-doors;
They must see something of the world!

Sing him a song, young men; remember, now, —
Not something too indelicate at first,
Lest it should shock the ears unused to songs
Except the kind they sing at morning prayers.

But even that
Has brought the color to his cheek; ah, well!
He 'll soon get over that, and when you 've sung
A dozen more, he 'll help you sing them.

What?
And must you go? It 's early yet. I see —
You promised to be home at nine o'clock;
That 's good! And if they question you, why, say
You went a walking with a pretty girl,
And they will laugh, and think you smart, and you
Can slip away, and none will be the wiser.
Good night! Good night! Be sure and come again!

Stand back, young men!
Here comes the boy again!
We knew that he would come! A taste of sin
Creates a thirst for more. What shall it be?
Pass the cigars; no, bring a cigarette;
He 'll take to that more easily, and it
Will work for rum and ruin just the same.
How pale he looks! Ha! ha! it makes him sick!
But never mind! He 'll try again to-morrow,
And soon will smoke a dozen (on the sly).
Go home and creep in bed, and say you 're sick
When mother climbs the stairs to wonder why
Her boy came home so late, and then forgot
To say good night. But come again!

Stand back, young men!
Here comes the boy again!
We thought we 'd lost him, but we might have known

There 's nothing makes a boy so bold as sin,
Nor weans his heart so soon from love and home.
Bring out the cards, and set the glass of wine
Where he can reach it should he so incline,
And laugh when he shall curse the holiest name,
And all things sacred turn to jest profane.

Stand back, young men! and give the boy a chance
In the front rank with those who miss the goal,
Who bury hope and faith, and kneel at length
Beside the grave of a remorseful past!

Stand back, ye tempters! Back, ye demons, stand!
And come, O heaven, with all thy shining ones
Arrayed for battle! Set them on the plains,
With flaming swords turning each way, to guard
The path of life of every boy.

God speed the day when men, with zeal aflame,
Shall join the shining hosts, to conquer Wrong,
And crown the Right with everlasting fame,
    And save the boys!
                      — Anna Barton.

HOEING AND PRAYING.

A good presentation of this bright poem can be made with the aid of a hoe. While representing Farmer Jones, let the speaker lean lazily on the hoe handle, but while speaking in the character of Farmer Gray, let him use the hoe energetically, talking as he hoes.

    Said Farmer Jones in a whining tone,
      To his good old neighbor Gray,

" I 've worn my knees nigh through to the
      bone,
   But it ain't no use to pray.

" Your corn looks twice as nice as mine,
   Though you don't pretend to be
A shinin' light in the church to shine
   An' tell salvation 's free.

" I 've prayed to the Lord a thousand times
   For to make that 'er corn grow ;
An' why yourn beats it so, an' climbs,
   I 'd gin a deal to know."

Said Farmer Gray to his neighbor Jones,
   In his easy, quiet way :
" When prayers get mixed with lazy bones,
   They don't make farmin' pay.

" Your weeds, I notice, are good and tall,
   In spite of all your prayers ;
You may pray for corn till the heavens fall,
   If you don't dig up the tares.

" I mix my prayers with a little toil
   Along in every row ;
An' I work this mixture into the soil
   Quite vig'rous with a hoe.

" So while I 'm praying I use my hoe,
   An' do my level best
To keep down the weeds along each row,
   An' the Lord, he does the rest.

" It 's well for to pray both night and morn,
  As every farmer knows;
But the place to pray for thrifty corn
  Is right between the rows.

" You must use your hands while praying,
    though,
  If an answer you would get;
For prayer-worn knees an' a rusty hoe
  Never raised a big crop yet.

" An' so believe, my good old friend,
  If you mean to win the day,
From ploughing clean to the harvest's end,
  You must hoe as well as pray."

HOW IT BEGAN.

Ten boys repeat this piece, taking the lines in turn.
The first boy holds in his hands "glass number one,"
which at the close of the recitation he sets down upside
down. Let the boys speak in concert the eleventh line and
the last one.

Glass number one, only in fun.
Glass number two, other boys do.
Glass number three, it won't hurt me.
Glass number four, only one more.
Glass number five, before a drive.
Glass number six, brains in a mix.
Glass number seven, stars up in heaven.
Glass number eight, stars in his pate.
Glass number nine, whiskey — not wine,

Glass number ten, drinking again?
Glass number twenty, not yet a plenty?
Drinking with boys, drowning his joys.
Drinking with men, just now and then.
Wasting his life, killing his wife.
Losing respect, manhood all wrecked.
Losing his friends, thus it all ends.
Glass number one, taken in fun,
Ruined his life, brought on strife,
Blighted his youth, sullied his truth.
In a few years brought many tears.
Gave only pain, stole all his gain.
Made him at last friendless, outcast.
Light-hearted boy, somebody's joy,
Do not begin early in sin;
Grow up a man, brave as you can.
Taste not in fun glass number one.

A MESSAGE FOR THE YEAR.

It would be appropriate if the speaker carried an old-fashioned hour-glass, or, possibly better, a flag with the number of the new year plainly marked upon it.

To every heart sore troubled
    I send this word of cheer:
You are gaining on the journey,
    You are nearer by a year.

Twelve months of storm and sunshine,
    Twelve months of joy and gloom,
Twelve months of work and waiting,
    Yet twelve months nearer home.

The far-off land is nearing,
  The waves roll toward the shore;
Behind the distance lengthens
  And shortens on before.

Each moment bears us onward;
  There is no time for tears;
Work, live, be patient ever,
  Through the swift passing years.

The "day-star is arising,"
  Earth's night is fading fast;
O, live the New Year, Christians,
  As though it were your last.
                    — *Mrs. H. F. Thomas.*

WE WON'T!

Let three boys speak this piece, each taking a stanza, and saying with much emphasis the last lines. At the close of each stanza, the other two boys add with much energy: " Nor we; indeed we won't! "

When I grow up, there are some things
  That I will never do,
And that 's as sure as grass is green
  And violets are blue.
I 'll never make my father sad
  Nor bring tears to my mother,
Nor give my sisters cause to say
  " We cannot love our brother."
I won't, indeed I won't!

I 'll never act with rudeness to
   Old folks.   I 'll never be
Unkind to any little child
   That comes for help to me.
I never will refuse to give
   A bit of bread and meat
To one who begs.   My horse and dog
   And cat I 'll never beat.
I won't, indeed I won't !

I 'll never swear; no gentleman,
   I'm very sure, does that;
I 'll never pass a lady friend
   And fail to lift my hat.
I 'll never drink strong drink, — O no,
   Nor ever smoke or chew, —
As sure as grass is always green
   And violets are blue —
I won't, indeed I won't !   — *Madge Eliot.*

AFTER.

Print in large letters on a long strip of white paper the verse: "Weeping may endure for a night, but joy cometh in the morning." Two girls step forward bearing this strip rolled up. They unroll it and hold it between them, facing the audience. Then they repeat the poem, taking the verses alternately.

After the shower, the tranquil sun;
Silver stars when the day is done.
After the snow, the emerald leaves;
After the harvest, golden sheaves.

After the clouds, the violet sky;
Quiet woods, when the wind goes by.
After the tempest, the lull of waves;
After the battle, peaceful graves.

After the knell, the wedding bells;
Joyful greetings, from sad farewells.
After the bud, the radiant rose;
After our weeping, sweet repose.

After the burden, the blissful need;
After the furrow, the waking seed.
After the flight, the downy nest;
Beyond the shadowy river — rest.

VOTE FOR ME, PAPA.

This speaker may carry a placard bearing in big letters
the words, " No License."

" Say, papa, how are you going to vote ? "
'T was a child's bright word, and he could
    not note
How the red blood mantled his father's face
And he clasped the wee one in a close
    embrace ;
But he prattled on in his childish glee,
" Say, papa, why don't you vote for me ? "

Out of the door strode the father fast,
And never a glance behind him cast,
And on to his place at the polls he went,
But the words the boy spoke were surely meant

By God above to follow him there,
For they haunted his steps like a mother's
    prayer.

"Vote for me, papa," the bells rang out;
"Vote for me," sounded the school-boy's
    shout;
"Vote for me," came from the rumseller's door
In the oaths he had never thus heard before.
At last, with a smile he whispered low,
"If I vote for my boy, I can vote only, No."

THE HARVEST TIME,

For a harvest concert this poem will furnish a pleasant
feature, especially if it is recited by girls, who come forward with arms full of autumn fruits and grains. The
stanza should be spoken by separate speakers, and the
last speaker should carry nothing but a Bible.

This is the gathering time of the year,
    And merry singing of harvest home,
And the signs of plenty and right good cheer,
    Ere the days that are dark and dreary come.
These are the days of a tranquil air,
This is the time of an answered prayer.

Was ever such gold as the golden grain
    Heaped in the fields for the needs of man?
Warmed by the sunshine, watered by rain,
    It pays for all care as it only can.
It has done its part, and its life it yields
To the harvest song of the clean-swept fields.

Meadows, and orchards, and rich corn-lands
  Are wealthy with fruitage of all the year;
And the world seems lifting its thankful hands
  For the needed blessings that aye are near;
The year is glad when it gains its prime,
And hearts are merry at harvest time.

Whoever is thankful let him come,
  With willing hands and a loyal heart,
And help in another harvest home,
  Where the Master calls him to do his part;
For he points to the whitened fields again,
And the harvests he loves are the souls of men.
               — *Marianne Farningham.*

THANKSGIVING.

Five children should speak this poem, each repeating the first four lines of a single stanza, and all uniting to say reverently, with clasped hands, " We thank thee, Lord!"

    For sun and rain and frost and wind;
    For shelter, health, and peace of mind;
    For winter's snow and summer's gold;
    For wealth of pasture, field, and fold —
      We thank thee, Lord!

    For the homestead's cheer and the nation's
      peace;
    For sorrows healed, for joy's increase;
    For friendship and for kindred love;
    For all the varied goods we have —
      We thank thee, Lord!

For all the ill that has not come
To desolate us, heart and home;
That unseen foes, that lurk and hide
To smite us, thou hast turned aside —
    We thank thee, Lord!

For patient love that spares us still —
Sinners, deserving only ill;
For faithful searchings of the heart,
And grace to choose the better part —
    We thank thee, Lord!

For kind, restraining, hindering power,
Holding us in the evil hour;
That thou hast saved from harm and fear
Our helpless souls through all the year —
    We thank thee, Lord!

A RHYME OF THE BLESSED SEASON.

Six children might speak this poem, each repeating one
stanza, and all joining in the last one. Each of the
children may bear a different Christmas emblem. The
list might appropriately be, in the order of the stanzas: a
bunch of holly, a Christmas bell, an armful of bundles, a
Christmas taper, a shepherd's crook covered with ever-
green, a Christmas star made from silver paper.

This is the blessed season;
   The blessed season brings
Gentleness and friendliness
   And all pleasant things.

The fields begin to whiten,
    The bells begin to chime;
Happy are the meek in heart
    Who honor the time!

This is the blessed season
    That opens every door
With help for the fatherless
    And gifts for the poor.

Every church is lighted
    For the blessed feast,
Every child is welcome
    From greatest to least.

The sheep are in the sheep-fold,
    The cows are in the stall,
Night is in the starry sky
    And God over all.

This is the blessed season
    And this the blessed day
When Jesus in the manger
    A little child lay.

And since he brought the good news
    We'll pray to him above
To look upon our human hearts
    And fill them with his love.
                    — *Dora Read Goodale.*

IMPORTANT TO DRINKERS.

The speaker should be provided with a number of bottles of the right size and shape to answer to the different kinds of liquors mentioned.   He should ta: i by an open window, and after taking up each bottle and telling about it, he should fling it out of the window with an exclamation of disgust, — "Bah!"   At the close he holds up a glass of clear water.

A man who drinks whiskey may feel awhile
    frisky,
  And paint the town brilliantly red;
But soon in the gutter with misery utter
  He will curse and wish himself dead.

A man who drinks brandy may feel like a
    dandy,
  As long as the smell's on his breath;
But soon in the tremens, snakes, bogies,
    and demons
  Will chase him and scare him to death.

A man who drinks wine may feel very fine,
  And play funny antics and shout;
But for it he'll pay with headaches next day,
  And die when he's young, from the gout.

A man who drinks gin with pleasure will grin,
  And have what he calls a good time;
Till with a red nose and dirty old clothes,
  He, homeless, will beg for a dime.

A man who drinks beer feels good for a year,
  And thinks it won't hurt him a bit;

Till, bloated and red, he goes to his bed,
   Or falls on the street in a fit.

But he who drinks water, as every one
     oughter,
   Enjoys to the utmost his life ;
He 's happy and healthy, respected and
     wealthy,
   And loved by his children and wife.
                     — *H. C. Dodge.*

THE BELL OF JUSTICE.

Good poems for recitation at meetings in the interests of our dumb friends are much in demand, and therefore this is inserted, although it is intended for older persons than the Juniors. It would add to the interest of the piece if a bell might be hung up as a part of the decorations of the room, having a vine in place of a rope.

Once on a time an upright king
   Hung in the market place a bell
Which all who were oppressed might ring,
   And thus their wrongs and sorrows tell ;
Receive the justice which they needed,
And all the rights the law conceded.

Now when, with constant calls and time,
   The rope had nearly worn away,
They tied the tendril of a vine
   To stop the progress of decay,
And give to all who might require
That justice which should ne'er expire.

One day a poor old wretched horse,
  Deserted in declining age,
Had munched and pulled the hanging vine,
  Attempting hunger to assuage ;
And ringing thus the justice bell,
Proclaimed the wrongs he could not tell.

Before the king the courtiers brought
  The hungry and neglected steed.
He ruled his owner should be sought
  And forced to keep him in his need —
Thus justice should protect the least,
And reign alike o'er man and beast.
                    — *J. S. Henderson.*

CHRISTMAS EVE.

While this is being recited in a clear, loud voice, let the accompanist play gently some appropriate music, which will remind the audience of the angelic chorus.

Calm on the listening ear of night
  Come heaven's melodious strains,
Where wild Judea stretches far
  Her silver-mantled plains.

Celestial choirs, from courts above,
  Shed sacred glories there:
And angels, with their sparkling lyres,
  Make music on the air.

The answering hills of Palestine
  Send back the glad reply,
And greet from all their holy heights
  The Day-spring from on high.

O'er the blue depths of Galilee
  There comes a holier calm;
And Sharon waves, in solemn praise,
  Her silent groves of palm.

" Glory to God," the sounding skies
  Loud with their anthems ring;
" Peace to the earth, good-will to men,
  From heaven's eternal King."

Light on thy hills, Jerusalem!
  The Saviour now is born;
And bright on Bethlehem's joyous plains
  Breaks the first Christmas morn.
                              — E. H. Sears.

HARVEST GLADNESS.

Three children should repeat this, each taking one of
the long stanzas. The couplets and the " Amen " at the
close should be said reverently by all **together.**

Praise be thine, eternal King!
Young and old " Hosanna " sing.
Thou hast blest us far and wide
At the beauteous harvest-tide.
Angel voices high are blending
In the anthem never-ending:

Praise for sun and praise for dew,
Praise for love forever new;
Praise for bounties richly shed,
That thy children may be fed;
Bread of Life, for all availing,
Vine the true, the never-failing!

Hear us, while we fain would render
Praise for mercies kind and tender.

Lord, 'tis thine almighty hand
That enwreathes the radiant land,
That the pastures doth enfold
In a royal robe of gold.
Shining vineyards, hilltops hoary,
Woods aflame, declare thy glory;
Thou hast hung the fruitage glowing
Where the orchard-boughs are blowing.

Feed our souls in thee confiding,
Keep our lives in thine abiding.

Old and young their music raise,
All things breathing chant thy praise;
Every season, every year,
Are thy tender mercies near;
Thou our Hope, our Help forever,
God of harvest, leave us never,
Till we reach our Father's portal,
Bearing homeward sheaves immortal!
    Amen.

        — *The Quiver.*

THE KING'S DAUGHTER.

It will make a pleasant reference to the international order of King's Daughters and Sons, if the child who speaks this piece wears somewhere the colors of that organization, — purple and silver, — and bears on the breast a large Maltese cross made of silver paper.

She wears no jewel upon hand or brow,
　　No badge by which she may be known to men;
But though she walk in plain attire now,
　　She is the daughter of the King; and when
　　　　Her Father calls her at his throne to wait,
　　　　She shall be clothed as doth befit her state.

Her Father sent her in his land to dwell,
　　Giving to her a work that must be done.
And since the King loves all his people well
　　Therefore she, too, cares for them every one.
　　　　Thus when she stoops to lift from want and
　　　　　　sin,
　　　　The brighter shines her royalty therein.

She walks erect through dangers manifold,
　　While many sink and fall on either hand.
She dreads not summer's heat, nor winter's cold,
　　For both are subject to the King's command.
　　　　She need not be afraid of anything,
　　　　Because she is a daughter of the King.

Even when the angel comes that men call Death
　　And name with terror, it appalls not her.
She turns to look at him with quickened breath,
　　Thinking, " It is the royal messenger."

Her heart rejoices that her Father calls
Her back to life within the palace walls.

For though the land she dwells in is most fair,
  Set round with streams, like picture in its frame,
Yet often in her heart deep longings are
  For " that imperial palace whence she came."
    Not perfect quite seems any earthly thing,
    Because she is a daughter of the King.
                    — *Rebecca P. Utter.*

THE BIBLE ALPHABET.

This exercise is to be given by twenty-six boys and
girls, or by thirteen, as you please. Each is to carry a
wand, at the end of which is a large, plain placard, like
this : —

```
+----------------------------------+
|                                  |
|               W                  |
|            Wisdom.               |
|                                  |
+----------------------------------+
```

The wand is to be held with the placard down, out of
sight, until each speaker begins, when it is to be turned
right side up and held high in the air for every one to see.
If only thirteen children are used, each child must have
two wands, one in each hand.   The first child will represent A and N ; the second, B and O, etc.   Either boys or
girls may be used, with the exception that K, of course,
should be a boy, and Q a girl.
  As soon as the children have taken their places upon
the platform, they sing brightly the following, to the tune
of " Christmas " :

      How shall the young secure their hearts,
        And guard their lives from sin ?
      Thy Word the choicest rules imparts
        To keep the conscience clean.

When once it enters to the mind
It spreads such light abroad,
The meanest souls instruction find,
And raise their thoughts to God.

The children then speak as follows : —

A. — The Bible is an *Aid* in all kinds of work, because it makes us more manly, and removes from our lives the sins that hinder our work.

B. — The Bible will fill any life with *Beauty* through the beautiful characters it describes, and the beautiful thoughts it expresses.

C. — The Bible gives *Comfort* to all who need it, because it shows the way out of all grief in this world, and a reward for all good men's sorrow in the world to come.

D. — The Bible always shows men what their *Duty* is, and gives them strength to do it.

E. — The Bible is a book that gives *Energy*. If you want to do things in this world, read the Bible.

F. — The Bible is a book full of *Fascination*. The more you know about it, the more you will be delighted with it.

G. — The Bible is the most *Gracious* of books. It is full of hope and forgiveness and kindness. And it makes gracious the people that love it.

H. — *Honor* comes from the Bible. The best way to get honor from men and from God is to honor God's Word.

I. — The Bible is an *Inspired* book, and so it is an inspiring book. It encourages one to do his best.

J. — There is no other book in the world so *Joyful* as the Bible.   There is no other book that will make men so happy.

K. — The Bible is the most *Kingly* book in the world, and it makes a true king of every man and boy that loves it.

L. — The Bible is full of *Love.*   No other book teaches so well how to love God and man, and how God loves us.

M. — The Bible is the one *Matchless* book of the world.   There is no book at all like it, or for a moment to be compared with it.

N. — In reading the Bible one is always finding something *New.*

O. — And at the same time the *Old* things in the Bible never grow stale.   We always go back to them with new enjoyment.

P. — The Bible is the most *Powerful* book in the world.   It has done more to make history than all other powers put together.

Q. — If the Bible is the most kingly book, it is also the most *Queenly.*   It makes a true queen of every girl or woman that loves it.

R. — The Bible is a mine of *Riches,* — wealth of character, wealth of thought, wealth of joy, and wealth of heaven.   The gold it gives is the only pure gold.

S. — The Bible stands for *Salvation.*   It tells about Christ, who is our only Saviour from sin.

T. — The Bible is true, and contains all the *Truth* that men need to know.

U. — Because all this is so, no other book in the

world is so *Useful* as the Bible, and no other book is useful in so many ways.

V. — The Bible gives a picture of all kinds of *Virtue.* You can find in the Bible a model for all good.

W. — The *Wisdom* of the Bible has never been approached. The world's wisest men have gone to it to be taught.

X. — There is no *Xcellence* that is lacking from the Bible, and no one can excel that does not love it and study it and obey it.

Y. — The spirit of the Bible is always *Young*, so that it is the book for our youth, and it will keep us young in heart although we become old in years.

Z. — The *Zeal* of the Bible is all for men, how it may make them better. Then let our zeal be for the Bible, how we may get others to love it.

In closing, all sing, raising their wands as high as they can, and looking up at them :

> Thy precepts make me truly wise;
>> I hate the sinner's road ;
> I hate my own vain thoughts that rise,
>> But love thy law, my God !

> Thy Word is everlasting truth ;
>> How pure is every page !
> Thy holy book shall guide our youth,
>> And well support our age.

Exact words on the placards : Aid, Beauty, Comfort, Duty, Energy, Fascination, Graciousness, Honor, Inspira-

tion, Joy, Kingliness, Love, Matchless, New, Old, Power,
Queenliness, Riches, Salvation, Truth, Usefulness, Virtue,
Wisdom, Xcellence, Youth, Zeal.

— Amos R. Wells.

KILLING FOR SPORT.

A bright addition to this recitation would be made by
two pictures, which may easily be found, one showing a
live deer, bounding along or drinking at a river, and the
other showing a dead deer, possibly hung up by the legs.
The speaker will hold up each picture at the appropriate
place.

> A pretty picture they make in the boat,
>   Drifting along by the river-side;
> He at the oars, while her fair white hand
>   Trolls at the stern in the ebbing tide.
>
> Hark! for a rustling sound is heard;
>   A timid deer has come down to drink;
> A gentle creature with great brown eyes,
>   Standing alert on the river's brink.
>
> A bullet whistles along the air;
>   It has struck the beautiful arching neck;
> The blood flows over the smooth, round
>   breast,
>   And begins the silvery stream to fleck.
>
> The creature struggles in agony,
>   Asking for help with appealing eyes:
> Half-rising, she staggers and falls again,
>   Then mutely suffers, and slowly dies.

What heart could have wrought the cruel
    deed?
    Who quenched the life of the harmless
        thing?
Alas! it was done by the fair white hand,
    And simply for sport — this suffering!

The picture is spoiled in the drifting boat;
    In the lovely foreground the deer lies
        slain;
The girl was thoughtless? But God forgive
    The woman who ever causes pain.

—*Sarah K. Bolton, in The Christian Endeavor
World.*

HEAVENLY TREASURE.

Three children repeat this poem, each taking a stanza.
The first speaker bears a placard which reads, in very large,
plain letters: " What I spent, I had "; the second, " What
I kept, I lost "; the third, " What I gave, I have."

    Every coin of earthly treasure
        We have lavished upon earth
    For our simply worldly pleasure
        May be reckoned something worth;
    For the spending was not losing,
        Though the purchase was but small:
    It has perished with the using —
        We have had it — that is all!

    All the gold we leave behind us
        When we turn to dust again,

Though our avarice may blind us,
　　We have gathered quite in vain;
Since we neither can direct it,
　　By the winds of fortune tossed,
Nor in other worlds expect it:
　　What we hoarded we have lost!

But each merciful oblation,
　　Seed of pity wisely sown —
What we give in self-negation,
　　We may wisely call our own;
For the treasure freely given
　　Is the treasure that we hoard,
Since the angels keep in heaven
　　What is lent unto Lord.
　　　　　　　　　　— John G. Saxe.

Used by courtesy of Houghton, Mifflin & Co.

THE LITTLE STREETS.

Draw upon the blackboard, or upon a large sheet of
paper, a map showing three streets converging in a city.
Letter the streets and the city very plainly, and have the
speaker use a pointer as if reciting a geography lesson.

　　" To-morrow I'll do it," says Bennie;
　　　" I will by and by," says Seth;
　　" Not now, — pretty soon," says Jennie;
　　　" In a minute," says little Beth.

O dear little people, remember
　　That, true as the stars in the sky,

The little streets of To-morrow,
  Pretty-soon, and By-and-by,
    Lead, one and all,
    As straight, they say,
    As the King's highway,
    To the city of *Not at All.*
       — *Annie Hamilton Donnell.*

THE FLAG OF OUR COUNTRY.

Five boys step forward, carrying flags. They speak in turn, each reciting one stanza. As the last lines of the stanzas (all but the fourth) are repeated, the boys should wave their flags gracefully together.

O flag of our country, bequeathed by our sires!
What love it enkindles, what work it inspires,
What hope for the future, what pride in the past!
O emblem of liberty! long may it last!

Of war-battered fortress and bravely-scaled peak,
Of battle historic, its mute folds would speak;
Of strong-moving column, of flower-strewn grave,
O emblem of liberty! voice of the brave!

In the North and the South, in the East and the
    West,
On live hero's standard and dead hero's breast,
O'er heads of the children, the heroes to be,
O emblem of liberty! flag of the free!

Long may it wave over the land it has won,
A gift from our fathers, through noble deeds done,

A trust to our children — O may it impart
Fresh love for the noble and true in each heart!

A gift to the children, the nation, the world,
A banner of progress o'er true hearts unfurled,
A plea to our manhood, a trust from the grave,
O emblem of liberty! long may it wave!
                    — Frank H. Sweet, in Forward.

CHRISTMAS BELLS.

Three children may recite this, each taking a stanza, and all joining in the last two lines of each stanza, which are a sort of refrain. If a soft-toned bell is struck in another room while this poem is being recited, it will add to the effect.

The Christmas bells, so soft and low,
Are ringing o'er a world of snow,
And tell us with their silv'ry chime
That gladness reigns in every clime.
The Christmas bells, so soft and low,
Are ringing o'er a world of snow.

The Christmas bells, so sweet and clear,
Are ringing for us, far and near,
And love-gifts swiftly wing their flight
From homes that gleam with Christmas light;
The Christmas bells, so sweet and clear,
Are ringing for us, far and near.

The Christmas bells! the Christmas bells!
How sweet the story each one tells

Of glinting star, of manger low,
Of love that sets the world aglow !
The Christmas bells ! the Christmas bells !
How sweet the story each one tells !
— *Belle Kellogg Towne, in Young People's Weekly.*

THE POOR MAN'S SHEAF.

This should be recited at a harvest concert, or in some similar gathering. Whoever recites it might bear a tin cup and a sheaf of wheat.

He saw the wheat fields waiting
All golden in the sun,
And strong and stalwart reapers
Went by him one by one.
" Oh, could I reap in harvest ! "
His heart made bitter cry ;
" I can do nothing, nothing,
So weak, alas, am I."

At eve a fainting traveller
Sunk down beside his door :
A cup of cool, sweet water
To quench his thirst he bore.
And when, refreshed and strengthened,
The traveller went his way,
Upon the poor man's threshold
A golden wheat sheaf lay.

When came the Lord of harvest,
He cried, " O Master kind,

One sheaf I have to offer,
  But that I did not bind.
I gave a cup of water
  To one athirst, and he
Left at my door, in going,
  This sheaf I offer thee."

Then said the Master softly:
  "Well pleased with this am I.
One of my angels left it
  With thee as he passed by.
Thou may'st not join the reapers
  Upon the harvest plain,
But he who helps a brother,
  Binds sheaves of richest grain."
                    — Eben E. Rexford.

SET IT DOWN, BOYS.

Let this be recited in a sprightly way by four boys, who
will each speak a stanza, and then unite in speaking the
closing stanza. With the last line of each stanza, let
the speaker go through the motion of turning a wine-glass
upside down. When the four boys make this gesture
together, it should be done strictly in time. With the
words, "Hurrah! Hurrah!" let the boys all swing their
right arms high in air.

If urged to lift the glass that tempts,
  In city grand or humble town,
Be he that tempts you king or czar,
  Quick, turn your glass, and set it down!

If those that ask you vex and tease,
  Perhaps condemn you with a frown,
Be firm, mind not the laugh and sneer,
  Quick, turn your glass, and set it down!

If health you crave and strength of arm,
  Would keep your hardy hue of brown,
Nor have the scarlet flush of sin,
  Quick, turn your glass, and set it down!

If in your trouble others say,
  " In sea of drink your sorrows drown,"
Look out, lest drowned the drinker be!
  Quick, turn your glass, and set it down!

Cold water, boys, hurrah! hurrah!
  Will help to health, wealth, and renown;
If urged to give these treasures up,
  Quick, turn your glass, and set it down!
                    — *Rev. Edward A. Rand.*

SOMEBODY ELSE.

Instruct the speaker to make a pause — a very distinct
one — before the " Somebody Else " each time it is spoken ;
speak it in italics !

Who 's Somebody Else? I should like to know,
  Does he live at the North or South?
Or is it a lady fair to see
  Whose name is in every one's mouth?

For Meg says, "Somebody Else will sing,"
　Or, "Somebody Else can play,"
And Jack says, " Please let Somebody Else
　Do some of the errands to-day."

If there's any hard or unpleasant task
　Or difficult thing to do,
'T is always offered to Somebody Else —
　Now isn't this very true?
But if some fruit or a pleasant trip
　Is offered to Dick or Jess,
We hear not a word of Somebody Else.
　Why? I will leave you to guess.

The words of cheer for a stranger lad
　This Somebody Else will speak,
And the poor and helpless who need a friend
　Good Somebody Else must seek.
The cup of cold water in Jesus' name,
　Oh, Somebody Else will offer,
And words of love for a broken heart
　Brave Somebody Else will proffer.

There are battles in life we only can fight,
　And victories, too, to win,
And Somebody Else cannot take our place,
　When we shall have "entered in."
But if Somebody Else has done his work
　While we for ease have striven,
'T will only be fair if the blessed reward
　To Somebody Else is given.

　　　　　　　　　　　— Union Signal.

ALL FOR TEMPERANCE.

Let each speaker carry some implement of his trade, thus, in order : a spade, a legal document, a rope, a bonnet, a book, a Bible, a frying-pan, a medicine bottle, a yardstick, an ink-bottle.

FIRST BOY.

Come, boys and girls, let 's each of us now
Choose the trade we will have when we 're women
    and men.
We are temperance soldiers, so, let what will come,
Our trade sha' n't encourage the traffic in rum.
I 'll be a farmer, but you never shall hear
That the hops that I raise ever make lager beer,
Or the apples I grow make cider to drink;
For vinegar and cooking, I 'll have plenty, I think.
And I 'll raise such fine crops to make men grow
    strong !
I shall just sing and whistle the summer day long.

SECOND BOY.

I 'll be a lawyer, but I never will lend
My counsel to bad men, a bad cause to defend;
And I 'll work without fees if I ever can aid
The cold-water army to put down the rum trade.

THIRD BOY.

I 'll be a sailor, then captain some day,
And sail o'er the ocean to lands far away.
But old Alcohol never shall step on my deck;
For where'er *he* is harbored, there 's sure to be
    wreck.

FIRST GIRL.

I 'll be a dressmaker, and milliner, too,
My dresses and bonnets will be wonders to view,
And I 'll do what I can that they never shall hide
The sorrowful heart of a rum-drinker's bride.

SECOND GIRL.

I 'll be a school-teacher, and do what I can
To make of each lad a good temperance man.
And I 'll teach all my girls to regard with a frown
Both tobacco and rum, and so put them down.

THIRD GIRL.

I 'll be a missionary, when I 've grown good and
    wise,
And teach the dark pagans the way to the skies;
I shall tell them the path that by drunkards is trod
Leads far, far away from our Father and God.

FOURTH GIRL.

I 'll be a housekeeper, to broil, bake, and stew,
And take care of my house as our good mothers do.
I 'll look after my household, and ever despise
Putting wine on the table, or brandy in pies.

FOURTH BOY.

I 'll be a doctor, and when folks are ill,
I 'll be ready to cure them with powder or pill;
But I ne'er will prescribe whiskey, brandy, or gin
To awaken old tastes, or the new to begin.

FIFTH BOY.

I 'll be a merchant, and keep a big store,
With large piles of goods, and clerks by the score,
And I 'll pay better wages than other men do,
If they 'll all be teetotalers, tried men and true.

SIXTH BOY.

I mean to fill an editor's station,
For his words reach men's ears all over the nation.
I 'll get good for myself and do good to others,
And try to help all as though they were brothers ;
No matter what fashionable wine-bibbers say,
I 'll teach *total abstinence*, the only safe way.
A member of Congress perhaps I may be,
Or even Vice-President they may make me.
And if *I* help to make laws for this nation of nations
Neither sailors nor soldiers will get *rum* with their
    rations,
And I 'll do what I can to lay by on the shelves
All the members who drink and make fools of them-
    selves.

ALL.

Brave and true boys and girls,
    Who will work with a will,
Can take a long step
    Toward removing this ill.
                    — *Union Signal.*

THE BIBLE.

This is a recitation for five children, who will recite in concert the first six lines, the remaining paragraphs being spoken by each in turn.   Each should carry a copy of the Bible, which he will hold out when he says " here."

Oh, never on this holy book
With careless, cold indifference look;
'T is God's own Word, and they who read
With pray'rful heart and reverent heed
Shall gain from each unfolded page
A blessing for their heritage.

If thou art sad, come here and find
A balm to soothe and cheer thy mind.

If thou art merry, here are songs
Meet to be sung by angels' tongues,
Meet to be sung by sinful men,
For whom the Lamb of God was slain.

If thou art rich in things of earth,
Learn here thy wealth is nothing worth.

If thou art poor, this precious mine
Hath countless treasures; they are thine.

Dost thou lack wisdom? Look herein,
And surely thou shalt wisdom win;
Wisdom to guide thee on the road
Which leads through faith in Christ to God.

— *Episcopal Recorder.*

MISSIONARY MOTHER GOOSE.

Provide for this speaker a very large tin pan, covered
with paper painted to look like pie-crust, with one section
cut out. Through this hole the speaker puts his hand,
and draws out, as he speaks, the various articles mentioned, — or as many of them as you can obtain. At the
close he holds up a Bible, which, of course, he does *not*
find in the pie.

> Little Jack Horner
> Sat in a corner
> Eating a very queer pie;
> He saw in a trice
> It held everything nice
> From the lands where the mission fields lie.

> From Ceylon came the spice,
> And from China the rice,
> And bananas from African highlands;
> There were nutmegs and cloves
> Sent from Borneo's groves,
> And yams from the South Sea Islands.

> There were nuts from Brazil
> All the corners to fill,
> And sugar and sago from Siam;
> And from Turkey a fig
> That was really so big,
> Jack's mouth thought, " It 's larger than I am."

> There were pomegranates fair
> Grown in Persia's soft air,
> And tortillas from Mexico found there;
> And there did appear

Grapes and grain from Corea,
And all of the things that abound there.

A Syrian date
Did not turn up too late,
He need not for tea to Japan go;
Tamarinds were not few,
There were oranges, too,
And from India many a mango.

" Now," thought little Jack,
What shall I send back
To these lands for their presents to me?
The Bible indeed
Is what they all need,
So that shall go over the sea."
— *M. E. Banks, in "Over Sea and Land,"*

OPPORTUNITY.

Three boys speak this, each taking one of the first three
stanzas, and all uniting on the fourth. The closing words
of each stanza, " Will it be one of you?" are also spoken
by the three in concert, as they stretch forth their hands
in appeal to the boys before them.

A judgeship is vacant, the ermine awaits
The shoulders of youth, brave, honest, and true;
Some one will be standing by fame's open gates,
I wonder, my boys, — Will it be one of you?

The president's chair of a great railroad maze
Is empty to-day, for death claimed his due;

The directors are choosing a man for his place ;
  I wonder, my boys, — Will it be one of you?

A pulpit is waiting for some one to fill ;
  Of eloquent men there are only a few ;
The man who can fill it must have power to thrill ;
  The best will be chosen, — Will it be one of you?

The great men about us will pass to their rest,
  Their places be filled by the boys who pursue
The search for the highest, the noblest, the best,
  I wonder who 'll fill them ; I hope 't will be you.
                        — Ram's Horn.

ROUND BY ROUND.

    This little poem may be spoken standing by the side of a ladder which has been placed at the back of the platform. The upper part of the ladder is hidden by folds of some gauzelike material. Do *not* place red marks on the rounds, as the third stanza would hint ; that is better left to the imagination.

    We cannot see the way ahead,
      But this we know each day,
    That heaven may crown the steep ascent,
      And hope is ours alway.

    This ladder-round we climb just now
      Is all we see, no more ;
    But smooth or rough, it lifts the same
      Up toward the King's own door.

And do we ask why on each round
   A print of blood we see?
A voice breathes low, " I go before, —
   The Christ who died for thee."

So up we toil from round to round;
   Some day will toil be o'er;
The last hard round of earth will prove
   The step to heaven's door.
              — *Good Housekeeping.*

A HINDOO WOMAN'S STORY.

This exercise should be given by four girls dressed in
Hindoo costume, which may be more or less elaborate
according to the resources at hand. The costume may
easily be imitated from pictures. It would be best for
some older worker to precede the recitations with a word
or two about the condition of Hindoo women before the
coming of the gospel.

THE HINDOO GIRL.

My father looks on his boys with pride,
And takes them oft with him to ride;
But with a different glance, I see, —
As I 'm "only a girl." — he looks on me.

And wondrous tales my brothers tell
Of temples in which the great gods dwell,
Of spreading trees with branches fair,
Of beauteous birds that cleave the air.

Oh, why may I never wander free
And all these sights and wonders see?

Oh, why must a girl be kept at home
And never abroad for pleasure roam?

THE HINDOO WIFE.

My husband's mother is harsh to me,
And yet I must obedient be :
Whatever she may do or say,
My part is simply to obey.

I wonder where my soul will go
When I am dead?   I fain would know.
'T is said that English women read ;
Oh, that must be a joy indeed!

I 've often heard my servants tell
That white men love their wives so well
That they eat with them, and 't is no
    disgrace
To be seen with them in a public place.

THE HINDOO MOTHER.

My pride, my beauteous boy, is dead!
Where, oh, where, hath his spirit fled?
In what humble form of a beast doth dwell
The soul of the babe I loved so well?

Oh, all is dark ! The gods love to destroy,
Else why in their wrath have they taken my
    boy ?
Oh, must I for ever from him part ?
Then nothing can solace this desolate heart.

THE MISSIONARY HAS CALLED.

I 've had a call from a lady fair
With mild blue eyes and golden hair,
And she tells of a wondrous God above —
A forgiving God, a God of love.

And she tells of his Son of wondrous birth,
Who came and dwelt on this sinful earth,
And died at last our souls to save,
And rose triumphant from the grave.

So wicked am I it cannot be
That the holy One could e'er love me.
I would believe, but oh, I find
'T is all so dark in my sinful mind!

I 've seen again that lady kind,
And she has prayed that I may find
Her God a God of love to me,
And that her Saviour my Saviour may be.

The blessed truth I now receive;
In Christ, my Saviour, I believe.
He listened to a woman's prayer:
A woman may salvation share.

— Forward.

"WAIT ON THE LORD."

This is a recitation for seven children. Each stanza leads up to a Scripture text, which should be printed in very large, plain letters upon a sheet of cardboard. This each reciter should carry in his hand, and on the conclusion of his stanza turn the card so that the audience can read the Scripture upon it. Let there be slight pauses after each recitation to permit this reading. In some cases it will be better to use only the principal portions of the Scripture indicated.

> Wait on Jesus, though of sinners
>   Thou may'st feel thyself the chief;
> In his precious blood he'll cleanse thee;
>   He will cure thy soul's deep grief.
>
>   1 Tim. 1 : 15.

> Wait upon him; in thy darkness
>   Rest thyself upon his love;
> Soon his light will break upon thee,
>   Soon his faithfulness thou'lt prove.
>
>   Job 11 : 16, 17.

> Wait upon him in thy weakness,
>   Though thou faintest by the way,
> Wondrous is the power he'll give thee;
>   He will be thy strength, thy stay.
>
>   2 Cor. 12 : 9.

> Wait upon him; take thy troubles,
>   Great and heavy though they be;
> Cast upon him every burden;
>   He'll support and comfort thee.
>
>   Ps. 55 : 22.

Wait upon him, though temptation
   Come against thee like a flood:
Jesus fought, and Jesus conquered;
   Jesus all his foes withstood.

Rev. 3 : 21.

And the soul that waiteth on him
   Shall in Christ's own strength be strong;
Nor can victory be doubtful,
   Though the conflict may be long.

Phil. 4 : 13.

For it is not thou that fightest,
   But thy God who fights for thee;
Thine 's the trusting, waiting, praising
   For continual victory.

2 Cor. 2 : 14.

— *The American Messenger.*

A LITTLE LESSON IN ARITHMETIC.

Four may take part in this short exercise, each giving one recitation. Just before each speaks, he should make upon a blackboard the sign of addition, subtraction, mulplication, or division, as the case may be. If there is no blackboard, use a sheet of paper and dark crayon.

ADD.

Add to your faith from day to day —
Knowledge and love, and you then will pray
As never before, for souls in need,
Who look to you, as for help they plead.
Add to your love the patience strong
That will still keep on, though the way be long.

Add to the pennies, nickels, and dimes,
And make them ring the pleasantest chimes,
As they send good news to the far-off climes
And to sad waifs here far happier times.
Add, and keep adding, from day to day;
In the mission cause 't is the only way.

SUBTRACT.

Subtract from your heart each selfish aim,
Let your gift be brought in the Saviour's name.
From the gold and silver subtract the dross;
Make the offering pure, for all else is loss.
Subtract all pride and all mere display;
In the work for Christ, 't is the only way,
And thus will he bless you, day by day.

MULTIPLY.

The seed that is sown must be multiplied,
And scattered and scattered far and wide.
The workers here and in every land
Should be increased to a mighty band.
The homes for the destitute and sad
Should be multiplied, and the world made glad.
By the help of all is the work increased,
From the greatest down to the very least.
The helpers should multiply each day
In the great world's work; 't is the only way.

DIVIDE.

Divide, divide, what you call your own,
And share with those that have never known

The light and love and the comfort true
That all your life have been given to you.
As freely as ye have received, then give,
For only by giving we truly live.
" Give a portion to seven, and also to eight,"
Is the Scripture word, and you must not wait
To see what somebody else will do ;
Be quick to give what belongs to you.
Divide your time and your money and all,
That you may answer the piteous call
That rings on the air from day to day.
Divide, yes, divide.   'T is the Christ-like way.
    — *Julia H. Johnston, in Over Sea and Land.*

THE BLOSSOM.

A pretty and telling accompaniment of this recitation
would be a small, common-looking box of earth in which
has been set some beautiful white plant like a lily.   Hide
the flower with a cone of black paper until the words,
" a blossom-wonder " ; then lift the cone.   With the first
line the child should drop into the box a few seeds.

Only a little shriveled seed —
It might be flower or grass or weed ;
Only a box of earth on the edge
Of a narrow, dusty window ledge ;
Only a few scant summer showers ;
Only a few clear shining hours, —
That was all.   Yet God could make
Out of these, for a sick child's sake,
A blossom-wonder as fair and sweet
As ever broke at an angel's feet.

Only a life of daily pain,
Wet with sorrowful tears for rain;
Warmed sometimes by a wandering gleam
Of joy that seemed but a happy dream.
A life as common and brown and bare
As the box of earth in the window there;
Yet it bore at last the precious bloom
Of a perfect soul in the lowly room, —
Pure as the snowy leaves that fold
Over the flower's heart of gold.
                        — *Henry Van Dyke, 1877.*

THE WARMTH OF A WORD.

It will add interest to the recitation of this piece if the speaker is a boy with a newsboy's outfit, carrying a bundle of papers under his arm. As he comes to the platform, he might cry some of the local papers — unless the entertainment is given in some place where this would not be proper.

'T was a day in the dead of winter,
   And the echo of hurried feet
Struck sharp from the icy pavement
   Of the pitiless city street.

Each passer was loth to linger,
   Though wrapped in a fur-clad fold ;
For the air was a-tingle with frost-flakes,
   And the sky was benumbed with cold.

The cimeter wind, in its fury,
   Bore down like a sweeping foe ;
The tempest was waiting the onset,
   And abroad were its scouts of snow.

Yet, amidst it all, with his tatters
  A-flap in the whirling blast,
A child who seemed born of the winter —
  A creature of penury — passed.

So tremulous were his accents,
  As he shivered and crouched and sung,
That the names of the mumbled papers
  Seemed frozen upon his tongue.

He paused for a bitter moment,
  As a wondrously genial face
Arrested his voice and held him
  With a pity that warmed the place.

" Have a paper? "   The kind eye glistened
  As the stranger took the sheet,
And glanced at the stiffened fingers,
  And thought of the icy feet,

Then dropped in his hand the value
  Of his fifty papers sold ;
" Ah, poor little friend," he faltered,
  " Don't you shiver and ache with cold ? "

The boy, with a gulp of gladness,
  Sobbed out, as he raised his eye
To the warmth of the face above him,
  " I did, sir, till you passed by."
— *Margaret J. Preston, in The Christian Union.*

LITTLE FOXES.

Use this as a dialogue, one speaker taking the stanzas referring to By-and-bye, I Can't, No Use in Trying, etc., and the other taking the contrasting stanzas. The first speaker may carry a branch of a grape-vine and pruning shears, and the second speaker may bear a musket.

Among my tender vines I spy
A little fox named — " By-and-bye."

Then set upon him quick, I say,
The swift young hunter — " Right-away."

Around each tender vine I plant
I find the little fox, " I Can't."

Then, fast as ever hunter ran,
Chase him with bold and brave — " I Can!"

" No Use in Trying " — lags and whines
This fox among my tender vines.

Then drive him low and drive him high
With this young hunter named — " I 'll Try."

Among the vines in my small lot
Creeps in the sly fox — " I Forgot!"

Then hunt him out, and to his den,
With — " I Will Not Forget Again!"

A little fox is hidden there
Among my vines, named — " I Don't Care ! "

Then let " I 'm Sorry " — hunter true —
Chase him afar from vines and you !

THE WINSOME LITTLE MAIDEN.

Let two girls come forward, one of them, who is to
represent Cheerfulness, being a very sunny-faced child,
and as young as possible.   The speaker will introduce her
to the audience in the following words.

Here is a little maiden —
   Who is she?   Do you know? —
Who always has a welcome
   Wherever she may go.

Her face is like the May-time,
   Her voice is like a bird's;
The sweetest of all music
   Is in her lightsome words.

Each spot she makes the brighter,
   As if she were the sun,
And she is sought and cherished
   And loved by every one.

You often must have met her,
   You certainly can guess.
What! must I introduce her?
   Her name is Cheerfulness.

A LITTLE BIRD TELLS.

When the speaker comes to the last line in each stanza, let him pause just before it, raise his forefinger and shake it slightly, then say in a half whisper, " A little bird tells."

Now, is n't it strange that our mothers
    Can find out all that we do?
If a body does anything naughty,
    Or says anything that 's not true,
They 'll look at you just a moment,
    Till your heart in your bosom swells,
And then they know all about it,
    For a little bird tells.

Now, where that little bird comes from,
    Or where that little bird goes,
If he 's covered with beautiful plumage
    Or black as the king of crows,
If his voice is as hoarse as a raven's
    Or as clear as the ringing of bells,
I know not; but this I am sure of —
    A little bird tells.

You may be in the depth of a closet,
    Where nobody sees but a mouse ;
You may be all alone in the cellar,
    You may be on top of the house ;
You may be in the dark and the silence,
    Or out in the woods and the dells ;
No matter — wherever it happens,
    The little bird tells.

And the only way you may stop him
Is just to be sure what you say —
Sure of your words and your actions,
Sure of your work and your play ;
Be honest, be brave, and be kindly,
Be gentle and loving as well,
And then you can laugh at the stories
All the birds in the country may tell.

THE CLOCK OF CONSCIENCE.

Get a loud-striking clock and place it, with some one to manage it, in a hidden corner.   Just before each child speaks, turn the hour hand around so that the clock will strike the hour, beginning with one.   The exercise requires, of course, twelve children, boys or girls, or both.

FIRST CHILD.

Listen to the clock !   The clock strikes one.
It is time that your sins should be over and done.

SECOND CHILD.

Hear the clock !   The clock strikes two.
Jesus is calling — calling *now* — for you.

THIRD CHILD.

Listen to the clock !   The clock strikes three.
Get ready now for eternity.

FOURTH CHILD.

Hear the clock !   The clock strikes four.
Now is the time of the open door.

FIFTH CHILD.

Listen to the clock! The clock strikes five.
Soon will the final hour arrive.

SIXTH CHILD.

Hear the clock! The clock strikes six.
" Put it off " is one of the devil's tricks.

SEVENTH CHILD.

Listen to the clock! The clock strikes seven.
Now is the time to decide for heaven.

EIGHTH CHILD.

Hear the clock! The clock strikes eight.
To-morrow may always be too late.

NINTH CHILD.

Listen to the clock! The clock strikes nine.
This moment, and this alone, is thine.

TENTH CHILD.

Hear the clock! The clock strikes ten.
To-day will never come again.

ELEVENTH CHILD.

Listen to the clock! It strikes eleven.
Choose while the chance to choose is given.

TWELFTH CHILD.

Hear the clock! For the day is past,
And there's not a day but may be your last.

ALL TOGETHER.

This is the clock of the conscience true.
Listen, and hear what it says to you.
                                    —*Amos R. Wells.*

CHRIST CARES.

To present this exercise, prepare eight large cubes of pasteboard, or blocks of wood. The six that are to be upright will each be painted with one letter of the word, "Christ." A peg will project upward from each, fitting into a socket in the one above, thus holding them all firmly together. The two blocks or pasteboard boxes remaining will be longer than the others, since they are to serve as arms of the cross, and each is to bear two letters, " C A " and " E S." They will be fastened to the upright by hooks, and the entire structure, when completed, will present this form:

```
            C
            H
        C A R E S
            I
            S
            T
```

Each speaker will hold up, as he speaks, his contribution to the cross, and when through he will hand it to the one who is conducting the exercises, who will put it in place.

First Speaker.— This " T " stands for " Teaches." That is what Christ does for me. He teaches me what is right and what is wrong. He teaches me how to be happy, and how to make others happy. Will you not take Christ for your teacher?

Second Speaker. — My letter, " S," stands for

"Saves." That is what Christ does for me. He
saves me from sin. He saves me from selfishness.
And he saves me from sorrow. Will you not have
Christ for your Saviour?

Third Speaker. — This "I" means "Invites."
Christ invites. He invites me. He invites you. He
invites us to everything that is good and beautiful
and happy. Shall we not accept his invitation?

Fourth Speaker. — My letter is "R," and stands
for "Rewards." Christ rewards us. He rewards us
for even the cup of cold water we give in his name,
and for everything we try to do for him. He rewards
us with happiness here and heaven hereafter. Shall
we not seek his rewards?

Fifth Speaker. — Here is "H," which means
"Helps." Christ helps every one that needs help
and asks him for it. He always helps at once and
in the very best way. Shall we not all get him to
help us?

Sixth Speaker. — This "C" stands for a beautiful
word, "Comforts." That is what Christ does — he
comforts us. Whenever we are in trouble, he comes
to us lovingly. He is ready to wipe away all tears.
Shall we not all rejoice in such a Comforter?

Seventh and Eighth Speakers (reciting in concert,
their blocks being first added to the cross, that the
whole word may be understood). —

> *Christ cares* — when fear and sorrow come,
> And all the world is cold and dumb.
> *Christ cares* — when we have done our best,
> And only failure stands confessed.

Christ cares for all our smallest woes;
With all our tears his pity flows;
In all our joy his gladness is,
And all our interests are his;
Yea, all our life our Jesus shares.
O blessed thought, — *Christ cares !   Christ
cares !*   *— Amos R. Wells.*

WHICH SIDE ARE YOU ON?

Let the speaker (who should be a girl) carry a poker in her hand to shake vigorously at the right time.

Come, children, and listen; I 'll tell you in rhyme
A story of something that happened one time.

There was war in the land, and each brave heart
    beat high,
And many went forth for their country to die;
But words fail to tell of the fear and dismay
Which swept the small village of W—— one day,
When the enemy's army marched into the street,
And their own valiant soldiers were forced to retreat.
Such hiding, surrendering, and trembling with fear!
When what in the midst of it all should appear
But Grandmother Gregory, feeble and old,
Coming out from her cottage courageous and bold.
She faced the intruders who marched through the
    land,
Shaking at them the poker she held in her hand.
" How foolish ! " her friends cried, provoked, it is
    true;

" Why, grandmother, what did you think *you* could
    do ? "
" Not much," answered grandma; " but ere they were
    gone
I wanted to show them which side I was on."

Now, children, I 've told this queer story to you
To remind you of something the weakest can do.
There is always a fight 'twixt the right and the
    wrong,
And the heat of the battle is borne by the strong;
But no matter how small or unfit for the field,
Or how feeble or graceless the weapon you wield,
O fail not, until the last enemy 's gone,
To stand up and show all which side you are on !
       — *Anna R. Henderson, in Our Youth.*

THE GIRLS THAT ARE WANTED.

    The girl who recites this may bear, hung from her neck,
a placard with the words, " Wanted, Girls."

    The girls that are wanted are home girls,
        Girls that are mother's right hand ;
    That fathers and brothers can trust in,
        And the little ones understand.

    Girls that are fair on the hearthstone,
        And pleasant when nobody sees ;
    Kind and sweet to their own folk,
        Ready and anxious to please.

The girls that are wanted are wise girls,
   That know what to do and to say,
That drive, with a smile or a soft word,
   The wrath of the household away.

The girls that are wanted are good girls,
   Good girls from the heart to the lips;
Pure as the lily is white and pure,
   From its heart to its sweet leaf tips.

I CAN'T, I WON'T, AND I WILL.

This is a recitation for three boys, who repeat in concert the first three stanzas and the seventh. The rest is divided up among them, "I Will" taking the lines describing him, etc. They must be drilled until they can come in very promptly. They should speak in harmony with their characters, "I Can't" drawling, "I Won't" harshly, and "I Will" brightly.

Three little boys in a rollicking mood
   Out in the snow at play;
Their hearts are light, for the sun is bright,
   On the glorious winter day.

Three little boys with shouts of glee
   Slide down a snowy hill,
And the names of the rollicking little boys
   Are "I Can't," "I Won't," and "I Will."

But play must cease, and a warning voice
   Calls out from the open door:
"Come, boys, here's a task for your nimble
      hands,
   We must have it done by four."

"I Will" speeds away at his mother's com-
    mand
  With a cheerful and sunny face,
And "I Can't" follows on with murmur and
    groan,
  At a weary and lagging pace.

But "I Won't," with a dark and angry frown,
  Goes sauntering down the street,
And sullenly idles the time away
  Till he thinks the task complete.

At school, "I Will" learns his lessons all
    well,
  And is seldom absent or late;
"I Can't" finds the lessons all too hard,
  "I Won't" hates book and slate.

So the seasons come and the seasons go,
  In their never-ceasing race,
And each little boy, now a stalwart man,
  In the busy world finds his place.

"I Will," with a courage undaunted, toils,
  And with high and resolute aim,
And the world is better because he lives,
  And he gains both honor and fame.

"I Can't" finds life an up-hill road;
  He faints in adversity,
And spends his life unloved and unknown
  In hopeless poverty.

" I Won't " opposes all projects and plans
   And scoffs at what others have wrought,
And so in his selfish idleness wrapped
   He dies and is soon forgot.

A GENTLE WORD.

A very effective way to present this is the following.
Let it be spoken in concert by a company of children, who
have been drilled to speak very distinctly and together, and
while they are speaking, let the organist play softly the
music of " Kind words shall never die," or some other
well-known piece appropriate to the thought of the reci
tation.

A gentle word is never lost !
   Oh, never then refuse one !
It cheers the heart when tempest-tossed,
   And lulls the cares that bruise one ;
It scatters sunshine o'er our way,
   And turns our thorns to roses ;
It changes weary night to day,
   And hope and love discloses.
A gentle word is never lost —
   Thy fallen brothers need it ;
How easy said ! how small the cost !
   With peace and comfort speed it !
Then drive the shadow from thy cheek —
   A smile can well replace it ;
Our voice is music when we speak
   With gentle words to grace it.

THE LITTLE ONES HE BLESSED.

The following poem, from "Little Knights and La-
dies," copyrighted in 1895, is used by permission of the
publishers, Messrs. Harper and Brothers. It should be
spoken, not by any of the children, but by some older
person addressing the children at the close of their entertainment.

I wonder if ever the children
  Who were blessed by the Master of old
Forgot he had made them his treasures,
  The dear little lambs of his fold.
I wonder if, angry and wilful,
  They wandered and went far astray,
The children whose feet had been guided
  So safe and so soon in the way.

One would think that the mothers at evening,
  Soft smoothing the silk-tangled hair,
And low leaning down to the murmur
  Of sweet, childish voices in prayer,
Oft bade the small pleaders to listen,
  If haply again they might hear
The words of the gentle Redeemer,
  Borne swift to the reverent ear.

And my heart cannot cherish the fancy
  That ever those children went wrong,
And were lost from the peace and the shelter,
  Shut out from the feast and the song;
To the day of gray hairs they remembered,
  I think, how the hands that were riven

Were laid on their heads when Christ uttered,
    "Of such is the kingdom of heaven."

He has said it to you, lads and lassies,
    Who spell it in God's Word to-day;
You, too, may be sorry for sinning,
    You also believe and obey;
And 't will grieve the dear Saviour in heaven
    If one, only one, shall go wrong —
Be lost from the cold and the shelter,
    Shut out from the feast and the song.
                    — *Margaret E. Sangster.*

THE SEVEN SISTERS.

The child that speaks this should wear, hung around her neck, a chain of pasteboard placards, on each of which is printed in large letters the name of a day of the week. All but one of these cards is gilded; that is colored gray and the speaker points to it at the close.

Seven sisters came my way,
Crowned with gold and shod with gray,
Traveling in single file ;
Each abode with me a while.
Each brought nothing in her hand
Save a passport to the land,
And the promise soon to bring
Each a present to her king.

When the first one left the door,
In her gracious hand she bore

Fairest gift of all the seven,
Incense made of prayers to heaven.
After her another sped
With a gift of wheaten bread.
Two a little garment took;
One a poem, one a book
Over which an ailing child
Half forgot his grief and smiled.

So in turn the sisters passed,
Each one laden, save the last.
Seven sisters came to seek
Each a good gift from the week.
Six returned with what they sought,
Something said or something wrought;
But the sister clad in gray
Was a little wasted day.
— *Ola Moore, in the Youth's Companion.*

HOW TO SPELL IT.

An exercise for three children. Let each carry one of
the letters, holding it up in plain view.

FIRST CHILD.

R is the *Ruin* the liquor will cause, —
The ruin of character, freedom, and laws.

SECOND CHILD.

U is *Ungodliness;* learn how the Lord
Has cursed the foul liquor in his blessed Word.

THIRD CHILD.

M stands for *Murder* of body and soul, —
Health, happiness, home, in the devil's control.

ALL THREE.

So *Ruin, Ungodliness, Murder,* all come
Together and help in the spelling of *Rum.*
                              —*Amos R. Wells.*

"THE PRETTIEST GIRL."

This poem, which originally appeared in *Harper's Young People*, is used by the kind permission of the publishers, Messrs. Harper and Brothers. It will add to the interest of this recitation, if the speaker has pinned to his coat a home-made valentine of the old-fashioned kind — a big red heart with an arrow stuck through it.

We had such fun on Valentine's Day
With the little girls who live over the way!
Teddy and I, and Jed and Joe,
Picked out the prettiest girls, you know,
And wrote 'em things about " Violets blue,
And sugar is sweet, and so are you ";
And only that Bobby said it was mean,
I wanted to write, " The grass is green,
And so are you," and send it out
To a girl we fellows don't care about.

But Bobby, he 's queer and does n't go
For fun, like the rest of us chaps, you know.
Why, who do you think he chose to be
His Valentine ? Now if I 'd been he,

I 'd rather have chosen — never mind ;
I 'll tell you about it, and you will find
That if ever you want a fellow that 's queer,
You 'll get him in Bobby, never you fear.

You see, we boys had all picked out,
As I told you, the prettiest girls about;
But Bob he said there was n't a girl
As pretty as his, and there was n't a curl
On any girl's head that could half compare
With his chosen Valentine's soft, fine hair ;
And he said her eyes were a whole lot bluer
Than any skies, and double the truer,
And that he was going to be her knight,
And take care of her always with main and
     might.

He would n't tell us his Valentine's name
Till the regular day for valentines came,
And mamma had hers, and sister, you know
(Of course from papa and sister's beau).
Then Bob he told us to come ahead,
And he 'd prove the truth of all he had said.
And where do you think he took us boys —
Hushing us up at the leastest noise,
And making us promise not to laugh,
Nor quiz him, nor give him any chaff ?

Why, he opened grandmamma's door: " See
     there ! "
He said.   It was grandmamma, I declare ! —

Grandmamma sitting and knitting away,
Sweet grandmamma with her hair so gray,
Lying all soft on her forehead in curls
Just as pretty as any girl's.
And I never had noticed before how blue
Were grandmamma's eyes.   It was really true,
As Bobby had said, that there never were skies
One bit bluer than grandmamma's eyes.

So she was his Valentine, he was her knight,
And somehow we all thought Bobby was right
When he kissed her hand, and cried in glee
" Dear grandma 's the 'prettiest girl' you see:
Of course I chose her instead of mamma,
For she, you know, belongs to papa.
But grandpa 's in heaven, and so I knew
That grandma must be my Valentine true."
                              — *Mary D. Brine.*

THE BRIGHT SIDE.

This poem first appeared in *Harper's Bazar*, and is used by the kind permission of the publishers, Messrs. Harper and Brothers. It should be spoken by a child who carries a pasteboard shield. One side of the shield is painted black. A streak of red forked lightning may be represented darting across it. The other side is painted blue, and in the centre is a bright gilt sun, with rays reaching out in all directions. The shield is turned at appropriate points in the recitation.

If one looks upon the *bright* side
It is sure to be on the *right* side —

At least, that's how I 've found it as I 've journeyed
    through each day;
    And it 's queer how shadows vanish,
    And how easy 't is to banish
From a bright-side sort of nature every doleful thing
    away.

    There are two sides to a question,
    As we know; so the suggestion
Of the side which holds the sunlight seems most
    reasonable to me;
    And you know, we can't be merry
    And make our surroundings cheery,
If we will persist in *coddling* every gloomy thing we see.

    There 's a sensible quotation
    Which will fit in every station –
We all know it — " As the twig is bent, so is the tree
    inclined."
    And the twigs of thought we 're bending,
    If to ways of *gloom* we 're tending,
Will be pretty sure to twist and dwarf and quite
    deform the mind.

    There 's a way of searching over
    The wide skies till we discover
Whether storms are on the way or the weather that
    we love;
    And the blue may fast be hiding
    Back of clouds which swift are riding,
Yet we know the blue is shining still and spreading
    far above.

And while that will last for ever
(For the *true blue fadeth never*),
The dark clouds must soon or later be dispersed and
    fade away ;
And the sweet " bright side " still shining
Will meet the eyes inclining
To watch for it and welcome it, however dark the
    day.

So, my friends, let 's choose the bright side,
Just the happy, glorious *right* side,
Which will give us wealth and spirits just as long as
    life shall last;
And the sorrows that roll o'er us
Shall not always go before us
If we keep a watch for *blue* skies and will hold their
    sunshine fast.

—Mary D. Brine.

THE BOOK OF THE YEAR.

The following poem, from " Little Knights and La-
dies," copyrighted in 1895, is used by permission of the
publishers, Messrs. Harper and Brothers.   The child that
recites this piece should carry a large book, beautifully
bound, whose pages she turns as she speaks, appearing to
be looking at them.   With the sixth stanza, however,
she looks up from the book, and from there on she speaks
directly to the audience.

Of all the beautiful fancies
    That cluster about the year,
Tiptoeing over the threshold
    When its earliest dawn is here,

The best is the simple legend
  Of a book for you and me,
So fair that our guardian angels
  Desire its lines to see :

It is full of the brightest pictures
  Of dream and story and rhyme,
And the whole wide world together
  Turns only a page at a time.

Some of the leaves are dazzling
  With the feather-flakes of the snow;
Some of them thrill to the music
  Of the merriest winds that blow :

Some of them keep the secrets
  That made the roses sweet ;
Some of them sway and nestle
  With the golden heads of wheat.

I cannot begin to tell you
  Of the lovely things to be
In the wonderful year-book waiting,
  A gift for you and for me.

And a thought most strange and solemn
  Is borne upon my mind :
On every page a column
  For ourselves we'll surely find.

Write what we may upon it,
  The record there will stay

Till the books of time are opened
    In the Court of the Judgment Day.

And should we not be careful
    Lest the words our fingers write
Shall rise to shame our faces
    When we stand in the dear Lord's sight?

And should we not remember
    To dread no thought of blame,
If we sign each page that we finish
    With faith in the dear Lord's name?
                    —*Margaret E. Sangster.*

FORTY CENTS A YEAR.

Before this recitation is given the leader of the exercises should tell the audience the shameful fact that the average gift of church-members to the cause of foreign missions is less than forty cents a year. The speaker will carry a contribution-box, plainly marked " 40 ct."

When our ever-living Saviour passed away from
    earthly eyes,
Sounded forth this great commandment from the
    eager, opening skies:
" Go ye, go ye, teach all nations, boldly teach them
    and baptize."

So they went, those men anointed with a power from
    on high;

So they went, to sneers and hunger, to the mob's
    vindictive cry;
Went to suffer racking tortures and triumphantly to
    die.

All their life was but one purpose, that the life of
    Christ should be
Spread abroad among earth's millions as the waters
    fill the sea.
So the heroes died, and, dying, left their task for you
    and me.

Children of the saints and martyrs, with all peace and
    plenty blest,
What obedience are we giving to the Saviour's last
    behest?
What desire, what self-denial, thought, and prayer,
    and eager zest?

In the stead of what the martyrs bore through many
    a conflict drear,
In the stead of homeless wanderings, bitter fightings,
    cruel fear, —
Ah, the shame! — we modern Christians give — *just
forty cents a year!*

Forty cents a year to open all the eyes of all the
    blind!
Forty cents a year to gather all the lost whom Christ
    would find!
Forty cents a year to carry hope and joy to all man-
    kind!

Worthy followers of the prophets, we who hold our
  gold so dear!
True descendants of the martyrs, Christ held far and
  coin held near!
Bold co-workers with the Almighty, — with our forty
  cents a year!

See amid the darkened nations what the signs of
  promise are,
Fires of love and truth enkindled, burning feebly,
  sundered far;
Here a gleam and there a glimmer of that holy
  Christmas star.

See the few, our saints, our heroes, battling bravely,
  hand to hand,
Where the myriad-headed horrors of the pit possess
  the land,
Striving, one against a million, to obey our Lord's
  command!

Mighty is the host infernal, richly stored its ranging
  tents,
Strong its age-encrusted armor. and its fortresses
  immense ;
And to meet that regnant evil we are sending — forty
  cents!

Christians, have you heard the story. how the basest
  man of men
Flung his foul, accursed silver in abhorrence back
  again?

"Thirty pieces" was the purchase of the world's
Redeemer — then.

Now — it's forty cents, *in copper*, for the Saviour has
grown cheap.
Now — to sell our Lord and Master we need only
stay asleep.
Now — the cursed Judas money is the money that
we keep.

But behold! I see the dawning of a large and generous day;
See the coming of a legion; read its banners: "Pray,
and Pay";
And I see the palm of triumph springing up along
its way.

These are they of open vision, open purses, open
heart;
Free from mammon's heavy bondage and the serfdom
of the mart;
Where the woe is, where the sin is, come to bear a
hero's part.

They have beaten out their coin into weapons for
the fight;
Glows the gold and gleams the silver in this legion of
the light;
Selfishness and sloth behind them, onward now for
God and right!

Lift your banners, loyal legion; swell your ranks from
every clime!

All the powers and thrones in heaven strengthen
    your resolves sublime !
Build the kingdom of your Captain on these latest
    shores of time !

             — *Amos R. Wells.*

A BENEDICTION.

    The recitation of this little poem would make a beauti-
ful close to a meeting or entertainment. It should be
spoken softly and in concert by a company of little girls.

The love of Christ befriend you,
The care of Christ attend you ;
Christ have you in his keeping
When all the world is sleeping ;
Christ be with you to-morrow
In pleasure or in sorrow ;
Christ help you in temptation
And every tribulation ;
Christ strengthen you for duty,
Give to your spirit beauty,
And comfort you with gladness
For every hour of sadness ;
Christ bid his angels serve you
And from all ill preserve you ;
Christ make you pure and holy,
Christ keep you meek and lowly,
Until with him in heaven
His crowning grace be given ;
The care of Christ defend you,
The love of Christ befriend you.

            — *Marianne Farningham.*

"BY THEIR FRUITS."

This may be recited by nine Juniors, each repeating one stanza, or by two Juniors, one giving the questions and the other the answers. At the beginning and the close let them repeat in concert Matt. 7:16.

What is the fruit of an ugly thought?
Ugly actions in passion wrought.

What is the fruit of an act of hate?
Remorse and misery all too late.

What is the sorrowful fruit of a lie?
Wrongs that grow as the days go by.

What is the fruit of a mocking word?
Angry feelings to action stirred.

What is the fruit that envy bears?
Discontent and a host of cares.

What is the fruit that worry brings?
Dread that poisons and fear that stings.

What is the fruit of covetousness?
Hearts that ever grow less and less.

What is the fruit of dishonesty?
Lives as wretched as lives can be.

What is the fruit of a headlong will?
Folly and failure and needless ill.

— Amos R. Wells.

OUR DENIALS.

The questions in italics should be spoken by one Junior. He will face three others, and these in turn will give the answers.

How do we our Lord deny,
Just like Peter, you and I?

By our words that twist and veer
Into byways insincere;
By our lying deeds that smile
Masking treachery with guile;
By whatever false may be,
For the living Truth is He.

How do we our Lord deny,
Just like Peter, you and I?

By the secret ways of sin
That we often travel in;
By the hidden things we know
We would not to others show;
By whatever dark may be,
For the living Light is He.

How do we our Lord deny
Just like Peter, you and I?

By our avaricious greed,
Envious thought and selfish deed;
By the cruel words we fling,
Words that rankle, words that sting;
By whatever harsh may be,
For the living Love is He. — *Amos. R. Wells.*

THE LORD'S PRAYER.

Seven Juniors may recite this, each repeating a couplet.
Or one Junior alone may recite the whole. Or the question
in each couplet may be asked by one Junior, and the
answer be given by another, making it a dialogue.

To whom should we pray? To the Father above,
Perfect in power, in wisdom, and love.

How shall the prayer begin? Start it with praise:
Hallowed His name through eternity's days.

What shall we pray for? His kingdom's full birth;
Pray that His will may be done on His earth.

What for ourselves? That to-day may be blest
With just the provision God sees to be best.

What for our past? That our sins He forgive,
Even as we in forgiveness may live.

What for our future? That nothing therein
Lead us and tempt us to folly and sin.

How shall our praying end? Praises again:
"God's be the glory forever. Amen."

— Amos R. Wells.

"CONSIDER THE LILIES."

This poem should be recited by five Juniors, each repeating a stanza. They may all carry lilies in their hands, and if you cannot get the flowers from the hothouse, you may make them from tissue paper.

"Consider the lilies," and what shall I find?
All things exquisite, pure, and refined.
Thus may my life be evermore seen,
Pure and holy and white and clean.

"Consider the lilies," and what shall I see?
Beauty as lovely as beauty can be.
Such is the beauty that God will bestow
Where souls, like lilies, in purity grow.

"Consider the lilies," and what shall I learn?
Nothing of God's wise creation to spurn.
Down in the blackness and grime of the ground,
See what a flower the Creator has found!

"Consider the lilies," and what is the gain?
Trust in the darkness, and patience in pain.
He who has room for the flowers in His plan
Surely will ever be mindful of man.

"Consider the lilies," and what if I do?
Then I must ever be faithful and true.
Joy like the lilies' will be my reward
If I but follow the word of the Lord.

— Amos R. Wells.

A PRESENT-DAY JOASH.

This will be spoken by one of the youngest Juniors, preferably by a boy.

King Joash won great glory
    In the days of old renown;
He repaired Jehovah's temple
    Where the house was broken down;
With carpenters and masons,
    And those that cleaned the floor,
He thoroughly repaired it,
    Till it needed nothing more.

I think we modern scholars,
    In God's own temple still,
May win the praise of Joash —
    If we but have the will —
By caring for the hymn-books,
    Nor scratching up the pew,
Nor muddying the carpets,
    As — well, sometimes we do.

For God is in His temple
    As surely now as then,
Although His form is hidden
    From eyes of mortal men.
Ah, if we once could see Him
    Within this holy place,
Who then would wish or venture
    Its fittings to deface?
                  — *Amos R. Wells.*

THE GOLDEN RULE.

Five Juniors may recite this, each repeating a stanza. Gild a foot rule and let it be passed from hand to hand, each speaker holding it as he repeats his stanza.

Measure your *words* by the Golden Rule:
　　Let no speech that you would not hear,
Nothing ugly or harsh or rude,
　　Fall from your lips on a listening ear.

Measure your *thoughts* by the Golden Rule:
　　Judging others gently and true,
Gladly forgiving and thinking no harm,
　　As those others should think of you.

Measure your *gifts* by the Golden Rule:
　　Wishes fulfill and needs relieve,
Largely, readily, generously;
　　Give as you would yourself receive.

Measure your *work* by the Golden Rule:
　　Labor for others as you desire
They should faithfully work for you,
　　Cheerful and strong, with a zeal entire.

Measure your *life* by the Golden Rule:
　　What you seek from the God above,
Measure back with an honest heart —
　　Constant service and constant love.

— Amos R. Wells.

CHRIST'S HAPPY ONES.

Eight Juniors will recite this, each repeating a stanza; or it may be given by two Juniors, one asking the question in the first half of each couplet and the other responding with the answer in the second half.

How are the poor in spirit blessed?
Theirs is the kingdom of peace and rest.

What is the blessing of those that mourn?
They in the Father's arms are borne.

What is the joy that befalls the meek?
They inherit unsought what others seek.

How are they happy that long for right?
They shall be filled with their chosen delight.

How are the merciful blest indeed?
They shall find mercy in their own need.

What is the joy of the pure in heart?
The vision of God in a place apart.

How does the peacemakers' bliss increase?
They are the sons of the God of peace.

Tortured for Christ, what reward is given?
Endless joy in the happy heaven.

— Amos R. Wells.

"WHOSE I AM AND WHOM I SERVE."

The Junior that recites this may carry in his hand a
model of an ancient sailing-vessel, a picture of which may
be found in any classical dictionary; or even a common toy
ship will answer.

> Dark and awful the night —
>   Rocks and breakers near,
> Ship in a pitiful plight,
>   Men in an anguish of fear.
> What is this that we hear?
>   What from the prisoner Paul?
> "Brothers, be of good cheer,
>   God will succor you all!"
>
> Thus, through the wrath of the sea,
>   Thus we race on our way,
> Lifting our passionate plea
>   Up through the wind and the spray.
> Then, with the dawning of day,
>   Lo, a glitter of sand!
> Lo, a welcoming bay,
>   And all come safely to land!
>
> Thus on the ocean of life,
>   You, O brother, and I,
> Caught in the storm and the strife,
>   Raise our pitiful cry.
> Who is it standing by,
>   Bidding "Be not afraid"?
> He, the Lord of the sky,
>   The sea and the tempest made.

Him if we loyally serve,
　His if we faithfully are,
Nothing our way shall swerve
　From the fixed and fortunate star.
See the haven afar!
　See the light on the foam!
See, just over the bar,
　Safety, and gladness, and home!

　　　　　　　　　— Amos R. Wells.

"A CONVENIENT SEASON."

Seven Juniors will recite this, each holding before him a placard bearing, in plain letters, the name of a day of the week. Before they repeat their couplets, they will recite in concert Acts 24:25.

Sunday.

Not to-day; it can wait a spell.
Surely to-morrow will do as well.

Monday.

This is a very busy day;
There's no harm in a slight delay.

Tuesday.

I'm really feeling dreadfully ill,
So not to-day; to-morrow I will.

Wednesday.

I'm not in just the right mood somehow;
I'll do it to-morrow; excuse me now.

Thursday.

I haven't given sufficient thought;
But I will to-morrow; I know I ought.

Friday.

I'm all tired out; but I'll rest to-night
And begin it to-morrow, fresh and bright.

Saturday.

I'll wait till Sunday; the wise men say,
"The better deed for the better day."

All.

Thus postponing from sun to sun,
Always *doing* and never *done*,
Brings at last to the judgment day:
What will the Lord, our Master, say?

— *Amos R. Wells.*

HIS NAME.

The following recitation is based upon the unfolding of the name of Christ in Isa. 9:6. The recitation is best presented by five Juniors, each giving a stanza, and each may carry a placard bearing in large type the word or words on which he speaks. Let all continue to hold out their placards till the piece is ended.

Let us name Him *Wonderful*,
　For He calmed the tempest's strife,
Healed the lepers, lame, and blind,
　Even brought the dead to life.

Let us name Him *Counselor*,
　For His wisdom rich and free,
Parables, Beatitudes —
　Never mortal spake as He.

Let us name Him *Mighty God*,
　Though He is the blessed Son;
Who knows Him knows God as well;
　They are one, forever one.

Everlasting Father, He;
　Nothing without Him was made,
And, through time till time shall end,
　All the worlds on Him are stayed.

Let us name Him *Prince of Peace*,
　For in Him mankind are bound
To their God whom they have wronged,
　To all men the world around.

— Amos R. Wells.

WHY? WHERE? WHEN? HOW?

This is a dialogue, to be spoken by two Juniors, giving
alternately the questions and the answers.

Why shall we give, that the giving may be
Joyous and liberal, hearty and free?

Give because Christ, and the Father in heaven,
All of our happiness freely have given.

Where shall we give, that the gifts we bestow
Just to the needy and worthy may go?

Give where the Saviour is; give where His cry
Sounds to His followers: "Pass ye not by!"

When shall we give, that the call and the need
Never may fail of our brotherly deed?

Constantly give, as the Father above
Constantly gives to the sons of His love.

How shall we give with the highest success?
How shall we give that our giving may bless?

Give with a reason, and also with care;
Give with humility; give with a prayer.

— *Amos R. Wells.*

WHAT WE NEED.

The questions should be spoken by one Junior and the answers by another. The first may be either a girl or a boy, but the answers should be given by a boy.

"What does a wise man need to wear,
      John the Baptist?"

"Simplest garments may yet be fair,
Raiment of skin and of camel's hair,
Fitness and service and little care."

"What does a wise man need to eat,
      John the Baptist?"

"Simplest viands are strong and sweet,
Locusts and honey are all my meat;
Glad content makes the fare complete."

"What does a wise man need for home,
      John the Baptist?"

"Over his head the bright blue dome;
Under his feet the fruitful loam.
God's love with him where'er he roam."

"What does a wise man need to say,
      John the Baptist?"

"Simple his words, 'Yea, yea; nay, nay.'
Strong his words, that all may obey.
Never a word from the truth shall stray."

"What does a wise man need to be,
  John the Baptist?"

"One that prays on his bended knee,
One that can ever his Father see,
One, though prisoner, glad and free."
                              — *Amos R. Wells.*

STUMBLING-BLOCKS.

This recitation will be given by four boys, each repeating
one stanza, and all joining in the final couplet. The
first three will carry cubes of pasteboard painted stone
color and labeled "Swearing," "Lying," "Conceit." The
fourth will carry a liquor bottle.

What are the stumbling-blocks? Swearing is one —
Meanest iniquity under the sun!
Over that stumbling-block reverence falls,
Over it dignity foolishly sprawls.
All that should awe and exalt and inspire
Ugly Profanity throws in the mire.

What are the stumbling-blocks? Lying is one.
Ah, the contemptible deeds it has done!
Honor falls over it, noble renown,
Good reputation — it throws them all down.
Kindliest confidence, neighborly trust,
Brotherly friendship, it drags in the dust.

What are the stumbling-blocks? One is conceit —
Many a snare it contrives for the feet!
Boldly we strut, and our fancies are high,
Loftily raised to the clouds in the sky.
Ha! there's the stumbling-block. Over we pitch,
All our proud fancies laid low in the ditch.

What are our stumbling-blocks? Worst of them all,
Over the bottle how many men fall!
Money and health and character go
Over the bottle and down into woe.
Honor and happiness, genius renowned,
Over the bottle they fall to the ground.

Lead us, O Father, along the life-way.
Keep us from stumbling and falling, we pray.

— Amos R. Wells.

SERVING, NOT SERVED.

This may be recited by one Junior, but it is better spoken
by four Juniors, each giving a stanza. The first may carry
a flower, the second a piece of coal, and the third a lighted
lamp or candle.

The flowerets bloom in meadows fair,
    Alluring to the eye,
And fling their fragrance on the air
    For all the passers-by.
They ask no blessing but to live,
And freely of their beauty give.

The pulses of the generous fire
Speed outward through the room,
And never of the labor tire
To banish cold and gloom.
The coal's warm heart beats true and free,
To heat the world for you and me.

The eager missionary light
No other living knows,
Save as in floods of lucid white
Forth into space it flows.
If once it ceases to outspread,
That instant, lo! the light is dead.

Ah, thus may I, in kindly ways,
Like fire and light and flower,
Fill all the minutes of my days
With love's unselfish power.
Thus what I spend shall yet remain,
And every gift shall be my gain.

— *Amos R. Wells.*

THE FOUR JEWELS.

This may be spoken by a single Junior, or, better, by four Juniors, who will recite in concert the first and last stanzas, and each recite one of the other stanzas.

A monarch sent four messengers,
  Each with a priceless gem,
And bade them seek four citizens
  And give the stones to them.

The first one found a toiling man
  Who bade him go away.
"I am too busy," said the man;
  "Please come another day."

The second found a jesting lad
  Who took the gem with glee,
And played with it a little while,
  Then tossed it to the sea.

The third one met an ugly man,
  Contemptuous and grim:
"Take back your jewel to the king,
  I want no gift from him!"

The fourth one found a wiser man
  Who took the precious thing,
And with a grateful, eager heart,
  From thenceforth served the king.

That jewel is a priceless truth
Sent by the King above.
Oh, gladly greet His messenger,
And take His gift in love.

— Amos R. Wells.

CHRISTMAS QUESTIONS.

The questions, in italics, will be asked by one Junior, who will carry a gilt star on a long wand. The answers will be given in turn by six other Juniors, who will speak promptly.

Who were the wise men, and what did they bring?
They were the sages that sought for the King.
Far, far they journeyed, from east to the west,
Bringing their costliest, purest, and best.

What was the star that directed their way?
Surely from heaven its glorious ray,
Showing and blessing the path that they trod;
What was the star but the shining of God?

Who was it really they sought from afar?
Lord of all beings, the sun and the star,
Maker of all things who all things controls,
Jesus, the Saviour and Master of souls!

How did they find Him, exulting, at last?
Simply by journeying, firmly and fast;
Simply by keeping their purposes true,
Doing the thing that they set forth to do.

We also seek Him, and how shall we find?
Only by getting a resolute mind;
Only by living the spirit of love,
Traveling onward and looking above.

When we have found Him, ah, what will He be?
Dearest of brothers to you and to me,
Strongest protector in any affray,
All through our lives, and forever and aye!

       — Amos R. Wells.

INDEX.

www.ingramcontent.com/pod-product-compliance
Lightning Source LLC
Chambersburg PA
CBHW020949030426
42339CB00004B/16